SQUASH!

SQUASH!

THE NEW PLAYER, THE NEW GAME

Adrian Goddard

ST. MARTIN'S PRESS
New York

Library of Congress Cataloging in Publication Data

Goddard, Adrian.
   Squash!

   1. Squash (Game) I. Title.
GV1004.G66   796.34'3   78-19585
ISBN 0-312-75432-9
ISBN 0-312-75433-7 pbk.

CONTENTS

To Peggy,
who made this book possible
and shared in every stage of its production.

ACKNOWLEDGEMENTS

I am indebted, first of all, to Adrian Zackheim, my editor, and Deborah Daly, the Art Director at St. Martin's Press. Benjamin Reeve came up with a first-class set of sequence photographs; his efforts were sponsored by the Bancroft Sporting Goods Co. The equipment for the display photographs in Chapter 2 was supplied by Ferons.

Special thanks to Arnold Moss, owner of the Broad Street Squash Club, who allowed us to use his facilities during our interminable photographic sessions. Thanks also to Lionel, Alex, and Bart for their patience and assistance.

The spectacular action photographs of squash stars which appear throughout the book were provided by Bob Lehman.

Finally, my thanks to Darwin P. Kingsley III, Executive Director of the U.S.S.R.A., and to his entire organization for their kind help and cooperation.

1

INTRODUCTION

Squash has suddenly gone public. Since 1973 the number of squash courts in the United States has doubled. Over five hundred thousand Americans now play the game regularly. Tournaments involving United States players appear on network television. Squash has left its elitist closet and become a truly popular sport.

This upsurge in popularity began with the recent recreation boom, when the search was on for agreeable forms of vigorous exercise. Investors began to offer a wide variety of facilities for participation sports. Even the most avid jogger or tennis player yearns for variety, and squash can provide it, day or night, rain or shine, winter or summer.

Until recently, newcomers to squash were intimidated by the way the ball behaved. Before the summer of 1977, "American" squash was played with a hard, fast-moving, solid rubber ball. Exceptional quickness was required to hit the hardball. Considerable strength was necessary to play that game effectively. The hardball alone was sufficient to deter most women who tried the game, and all but the most committed of males usually chose a less daunting form of exercise.

Sharif Khan during the final match of the North American Open in 1977 when he beat Geoff Hunt of Australia.

1

The United States Squash Racquets Association, responding to pressure from all sides, abandoned the hardball, and "American" squash is now played with a hollow "70-plus" rubber ball. It is softer, bounces higher, weighs less, and travels more slowly than its predecessor. Accordingly, the new squash game is easier for the beginning player. Rallies tend to last longer, as the ball is easier to return, and a short squash game now has an even greater exercise value. The risk of injury on the squash court—marginal though it was—has been reduced.

The streamlined and fashionable sport which squash has become is the most recent incarnation of a traditional four-wall racquet game with a long, venerable history. While its origins are somewhat uncertain, it seems that toward the end of the eighteenth century, inmates of the Fleet Prison in London bashed a ball around outdoors in the prison yard. News of the matches at Fleet spread, and bevies of society folk came to watch. The spectators were fascinated by the novelty of the game, and they recognized its potential as a vigorous, though decorous, activity for young men.

"Rackets" was born, and somehow found its way to the Harrow School. It arrived between 1815 and 1820. The only real difference from the original prison game was that rubber, rather than wood, began to be used for the balls. There were only a handful of places at Harrow suitable for rackets—"The Corner" was the favorite— and as the century progressed and the game took hold, they were in almost constant use. Pupils eager to improve their skills at rackets when the courts were busy devised a softer ball that was less likely to damage school property when used outside the designated areas. The version of rackets played with the softer ball put more emphasis on physical conditioning and mental discipline. This alternative game came to be known as squash.

In 1850, rackets or "harder" was given a separate home when two roofless courts were especially constructed for it. Squash and rackets now had distinct identities. In 1864, the process was completed with the building of the first four squash courts. The school's administrators promoted squash at the expense of rackets for reasons that still apply. More students got more exercise more safely in a smaller space for less money. Apart from the scoring system and the common concept of an indoor, four-wall racquet sport, the two games wound up miles apart.

A rackets court measures 60 by 30 feet, the squash court 32 by 18½ feet. The floor of a rackets court is usually stone, a squash court's wooden. Rackets court walls are black and unplastered, squash court walls white and plastered. The rackets racquet is bigger and stronger, and hits a solid white ball, rather than a softer green one with air in it. Rackets is a hazardous game of great speed which requires fast reflexes and highly developed racquet skills, but very little strategy. Squash is much more civilized, and when it got started, rackets went back to the woods.

By the 1890s, squash had found its way to America, and taken hold in parallel American institutions: private schools, Ivy League colleges, and exclusive university clubs. From its introduction in the United States, squash was established as an elitist gentleman's game.

The gentleman's game as played by two champions of 1955, Ernie Howard and Henri Salaun.

Over the next twenty years, squash developed separately on both sides of the Atlantic. The American game, which retained more of the elements of traditional "rackets," bore less and less resemblance to the English game. In 1907, the United States Squash Racquets Association was formed, and in 1929, the English Squash Rackets Association (later the International Federation) followed. The natural development of squash was halted, and each side became entrenched in defense of a quite different version of the same sport. The die was cast—and the possibility of international squash competition was precluded for nearly fifty years.

The game's commercial potential was first grasped in England after World War II. A parallel growth began later in America, culminating in the arrival of the new ball. It has opened doors to an even wider public, and to the possibility of some rapprochement between the International Federation (for the English ball) and the American authorities. Unfortunately, each side is still at the stage where meaningless traditions of separate administration are objects of pride. Money and public interest may eventually cure what is left of the schism, but the rift thus far remains. For the time being, the 70-plus ball is harder and faster than the English one, but it shares many more of its characteristics than did its predecessor. Now, at last, players of all levels can be successful with both balls.

Squash's privileged background is one of the keys, perhaps, to its unique appeal. There is a noble tradition of fair play, which is still upheld. It is bad form to take any unfair advantage in squash— to yell at your opponent, the referee, or even yourself. Physical contact, apart from a blithe handshake before and after the match, is not part of the game. It is an art to disguise all trace of emotion from your opponent while you're playing, but always remain courteous. So squash is the perfect game not only for competitors but also for those looking for a congenial form of exercise. Whether you win or lose, you'll always have the satisfaction of a good workout knocking a little rubber ball about.

Because of its great subtlety and constantly changing aspect, squash, like any other great sport, can be seen as an allegory of life, and this, in part, accounts for its compulsive quality. It has been called "chess for athletes" with some justice.

These niceties aside, your only obligation is to enjoy the game, for whatever reason and at whatever level you play. The only formalities are the booking of a court and the finding of an opponent. If you are a member of a club, you can usually arrange a game in two short phone calls. Squash, as played in cities these days, is streamlined to such an extent that a half hour of vigorous playing at lunchtime, which provides at least a day's worth of exercise, can still leave you time for a sandwich.

On the other hand, if you want to hang around after the game to grumble about your backhand, you'll have plenty of opportunity. Squash players usually can't say enough about each other's form—few of them can adequately express their theories on the court, which leaves plenty of material for the locker room.

Through all this there is the feeling of tradition, of inheriting a game that has had its heroes, its performances, to which the current generation may aspire. This is not a game such as racquetball, deliberately simplistic, imposed upon society according to a businessman's carefully constructed formula. Squash has an idiosyncratic beauty, a noble past, and an exciting future. Now is the perfect time to begin the game. Squash represents the best of city life, constructed for you to take only what you want from it. It is available to everyone, young and old, men, women and children. It will keep you happy and make you healthy.

The purpose of this book is first to acquaint you with the game, to explain the basic skills. As the book progresses, you will be led through the more complicated techniques with the aid of flip-through pictures which will break each stroke down to its components, and give you a sense of the rhythm essential to good form and effective play. Later chapters expound on the finer points of squash and the discipline required to win consistently. The book closes with a survey of recent changes in the game, and some words of advice for newcomers to squash. There is also a discussion of opportunities for competition and a look at the future of the game.

To help you develop the various strokes and techniques, the Appendix provides a selection of drills designed to imitate the game situation. The Appendix also outlines the official rules of the game and features a list of squash facilities currently available in the United States.

The star shots, which appear throughout most of the book, should provide some context for the written advice, as well as illustrating the grace and drama of top level play.

In keeping with the modern squash market, special attention is paid to the thousands of tennis players who are now trying out squash for the first time. Familiarity with any court or racquet sport is a considerable advantage to the squash novice, so squash is a natural for tennis players who are looking for a year-round racquet game. Weather conditions don't dictate your playing time, the racquet is already familiar, and in squash (as opposed to tennis) you can really slug the ball. There are far fewer inhibitions when you're hitting a ball against a wall and, since the squash court is enclosed, the ball can't escape so easily.

Although up to forty percent of the members at many commercial squash clubs are women, none of the recent books on the game have paid much attention to the woman's point of view. This book is frankly intended to foster interest in squash among prospective female players. The technique chapters which follow are written with women in mind, and the chapter which highlights the differences between men's and women's squash was written in consultation with Heather McKay, the world's leading female squash player.

So, keep this book by you whether you're male or female. It will serve as a comprehensive introduction to one of the world's most rewarding games. A careful reading of the technique chapters (along with some assiduous practice) might be more valuable than time spent with a squash pro—who has bad days, and who might be dumb or uninterested in the first place.

But whether or not you choose to invest in professional lessons, this book will provide a unique insider's view of this fascinating game whose principles are so easy to grasp, but so difficult to master.

Even the very best players don't always know what's going on. Mohibullah and Gul Khan (foreground) playing doubles with Stu Goldstein and Victor Niederhoffer.

2

BEGINNING TO PLAY

If you think squash might be the game for you, then you must first decide where to play. It's easier if the club you use at the beginning becomes your regular club (after you're hooked), so you should shop for the appropriate one right at the start.

Basically, there are three ways to play squash as an adult: as a member of a YMCA, a private club, or a public club. Although your first criterion will probably be convenient location, the three different types of club have different things to offer which should be considered as well.

YMCA prices are usually the lowest, but the courts are often jammed, the facilities are spartan, and rarely is there any kind of professional service or equipment shop.

To join a private club, you'll have to secure enough members' signatures or prove that you went to the right university before even producing your checkbook. Then there will be an initiation fee that can be anything up to $1000, plus first year dues, which could be an extra $1500 or more. Court fees may be less, but tuition and equipment costs will usually be more than at a public club. A private club generally offers a more intimate atmosphere

The lobby of an impressive new public facility: the Broad Street Squash Club in Lower Manhattan. (Photo by Benjamin Reeve.)

than a Y or a public club, particularly if you're on the inside of one of the inevitable cliques, and the pace is more leisurely. However, there are precious few beginners. The great majority of private clubs members have learned their squash, know they like it, and are happy to pay dearly for their privacy.

Public clubs usually fall between Y's and private clubs in cost and services provided. The pros usually charge about the same for lessons as at private clubs, but will probably have a great deal more experience with beginners. Annual dues run from $35 to about $100, and there are often reduced rates for juniors and families. Court fees usually run up a scale, from off-peak time (weekends, late evenings, mid-mornings) at about $5 to $12 per court per hour, to peak time where prices run from $8 to $25 per hour.

Pro shops at public clubs generally have a better selection of equipment than they do at private clubs, for less money. They can't afford to be too expensive, because of the obvious competition from sporting goods stores.

All in all, the best course for the average beginner is to try the game at a commercial public club, and if everything works out, to join it. Public clubs are the only facilities designed with the new player in mind, and all the services you'll need are arranged in one place.

Most public clubs will make your first encounter with squash as informal and unpressured as they can. The enormous number of new·customers for the squash business has made most of the commercial facilities adept at public relations, and common sense tells them that strangers to the game should have a painless introduction to it. When you walk into one of the spanking new facilities, don't be misled by appearances. You'll be shown around the club and you should feel like a customer rather than a nuisance. Check out the amenities and the ambience of the place—you won't want to spend much time there if the atmosphere is uncomfortable.

In most big cities, squash clubs compete seriously for customers, since it's a buyer's market. If one place doesn't have something you want—a weight room, sauna bath, English and/or doubles courts, or whatever—the chances are another one will. Wherever you go, be sure that there's air-conditioning for the summer months. That's not an extra, it's essential.

With a little luck, you'll be able to find a conveniently located club to suit your needs and tastes on first inspection. But don't sign anything until you've asked a few pointed questions. Don't be ashamed to ask away; if the management seems evasive, you have good reason to be suspicious.

How many members are there? The answer is important. A large membership justifies a certain amount of confidence in the services provided by the club, and also means you're more likely to find compatible playing partners. But if the membership seems disproportionately large, especially if the price is low, watch out. Check court availabilities for the times you want to play. Ask how far in advance you can book. There's nothing worse than coughing up a membership fee only to find you have to struggle to get a court.

One good way of gaining inside intelligence about a place is by engaging its members in conversation. If they like the club, the chances are they'll be loyal to it, and if they look reasonable, then you'll have some valuable information.

Is the professional approachable, or is he or she sitting on cloud nine in a white track-suit dreaming of the world championships? Ask to be introduced. Find out what his or her credentials are. Make him sell himself. Ask when he's available and how much he costs. Rates for individual lessons vary from about $10 to $50 per hour, depending upon reputation and credentials.

Try out the game before you join. Many clubs will offer you an introductory clinic. Most charge for the service, but it's worth it. Your best course is probably to experiment on your own and get some idea of how the game works before taking a lesson. But either way, you'll get to try the game before you part with too much money.

Check the pro shop. A good test is to ask how much it would cost to set a beginner up with the basic equipment: a comfortable pair of shoes, a racquet that won't fall to pieces, and a ball. If they can do it for $30 to $40, fine. If it's $50 or more, go to a sporting goods store or another club, because this one is trying to rip you off. Public clubs usually put an extra mark-up on their equipment prices in exchange for the convenience and superior advice they provide. But some of them go too far. Also, find out if they string racquets on the premises and how long it takes. It's infuriating to be prevented from playing by a chronically slow repair shop.

How much mixing is there between members? What kind of people frequent the club: business people, artists, secretaries, house-wives, singles? Would you be comfortable with them?

What kind of partner service do they have? If you join on your own, you're going to need people of a similar caliber to play with. If you join with a friend, he or she may be a lot worse or a lot better, or you might get sick of the same opponent week after week. A good matchmaking service can easily be the key to your enjoyment of a squash club.

On the basis of all the information you collect, ask yourself if it's worth it. Do you need the expensive extras? When assessing the cost of playing at a public club, don't forget the court fees. If the membership fee is low, the court fees may be high. If it looks like you'll be an enthusiast, it's obviously better to pay more for membership and less for court time. Ask the man behind the counter whether it's likely that court fees will be raised during the term of your membership.

If you're satisfied with the answers to all your questions and you've tried out the game, then join up. The next step is to choose your equipment. There's plenty to consider. We'll start from the ground and work up.

EQUIPMENT

Footwear.   Your shoes should provide plenty of cushioning, particularly for the ball of the foot and toes. They should be light and flexible, providing enough lateral support to prevent turned ankles.

When you're buying shoes, bring squash socks with you. Squash shoes should fit snugly, so don't buy large because you think your socks will fill up the spaces. Tennis shoes may seem sufficient at first, but you'll soon realize that they're too heavy and lack lateral support. Running shoes are better, so long as the padding and tread are not too exaggerated. Converse, Adidas, Puma, Head, Dunlop, and Pony are among the better brand names. Patrick manufactures a shoe specifically designed for squash, "The Copenhagen," which is excellent but expensive.

You can't play squash if your feet are blistered and, assuming that your shoes fit properly, you should be able to avoid blisters by choosing the right pair of socks. Be sure that your socks are thick, soft, snug (but not tight), and absorbent. Even the ideal sock will cause blisters if it's wet, so make sure that your socks are dry when you go on the court.

Shorts.   They should allow uninhibited movement; tennis shorts are too restricting. Running shorts or skirts are better (unless they're long and floppy).

Shirts.   More or less the same goes for the shirt, which should be light, absorbent, and sufficiently loose to be comfortable while you play. Pure nylon is not a good material for socks, skirts, shorts, or shirts.

Racquets.   There is a large range of weights, makes, string materials, and prices to choose from. Weights range from ladies' racquets, which are lighter than English weight racquets, to Australian weight racquets, 70-plus racquets, and old American hardball racquets, which are the heaviest. An English weight racquet may be too light for some 70-plus players, while the old hardball racquet is probably too heavy. Generally speaking, a beginner will want to buy light and stay there, or move to a heavier racquet as strength and skills improve. Another principal influence in the choice of racquet for a beginner should be price. Don't start out with a desperately expensive racquet, nor with a dirt cheap one. At the beginning you'll be hitting the walls too much for either to last you too long. The sophisticated selling points of expensive frames are irrelevant to someone beginning the game, who is capable at any time of reducing the most elite piece of wood to splinters. Really cheap racquets break so easily they can be dangerous.

The best policy is to buy a low-priced model from a reputable manufacturer. Some of the biggest and best brand names are Bancroft, Grays, Dunlop, Cleaves, Slazenger, Ascot, and Garcia. You'll still have plenty of choice about handles (round or square, long or short), grips (leather or terry cloth), shafts (rigid, bamboo, or even metal), different shaped heads, and, of course, different weights. Buy whatever feels most comfortable, and try some out before you do so. Your club will probably have racquets for rent. When testing a racquet, swing it hard—backhand and forehand—as though you mean business. A quick glance at the display shelf will not help you judge how the weight and grip of a particular racquet will suit you.

One thing to watch for: since the recent changeover to 70-plus squash, many retailers have been stuck with semi-obsolete heavy hardball racquets. By offering them at (apparently) bargain prices, they have lured many people into purchases they later regret. Make sure you know what you're buying. Heavy, bulky hardball racquets can be a severe liability in 70-plus squash.

As for stringing, nylon is the cheapest and strongest, and therefore the most appropriate for the beginner. The better grades of

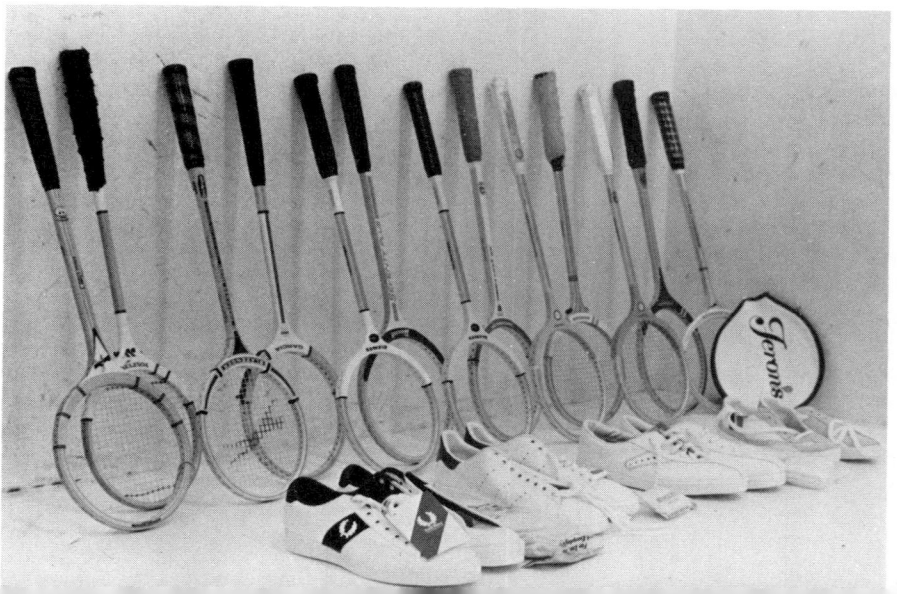

nylon, such as Blue Star, imitate the characteristics of gut and are a good compromise both in quality and price. Gut itself has two basic advantages over synthetic strings: it doesn't get shiny and slippery and it retains a slightly rough surface which allows better control of "slice," "cut," and other advanced effects. A frayed, well-worn gut racquet indicates seriousness in a squash player. Confidence, and hence performance, is often improved by a little equipment snobbery.

If you buy an unstrung racquet, you'll have to choose not only string materials, but also string tension. Standard tension is between thirty-four and forty pounds. A tightly strung racquet will deliver greater "punch," but you won't find this extra power very useful until your stroke is precise and extremely well timed. Generally, a more advanced player will tend to string his racquet more tightly.

Accessories.   In addition to the basic equipment, you'll also have a range of extras to consider. There is no reason to wear a glove unless avoiding a few honest callouses is more important to you than a large amount of control. When you start playing, your racquet hand will be soft and susceptible to blisters, but that won't last long. Replace terry cloth grips when they seem rough or slippery. Sweatbands are useful, particularly on the racquet arm, to prevent your grip from becoming moist and slippery. If your hair is long, a head-

< A wide range of squash equipment—including racquets, clothing, shoes, and accessories available at better sporting goods stores and pro shops. (Courtesy of Ferons.) Left to right (prices are approximate): hand exerciser, $2.50; eye/temple guard, $2.50; headband, $1.00; eyeglass holder, $1.50; grip tape, $1.50; warmup suit, $55.00.

< The rather bulkier racquet on the extreme left—the Garcia "Whipstroke," $30.00 (frame)—is an example of the obsolete hardball racquet. Don't invest in one of these unless you intend to play the old hardball game. The other racquets are designed for International ("softball") and 70-plus squash—and this is just a sampling of the choices. From left to right: the Yoneyama, $20.00 (prestrung); the Slazenger "Firepower," $17.00 (prestrung); the Garcia "240," $30.00 (frame); the Cleaves "Conquest," $26.00 (frame); the Bancroft "Seventy-Plus," $30.00 (frame); the Cleaves "Classic," $26.00 (frame); the Gray's "Matchmaster," $30.00 (frame); the Lady Gray, $28.00 (frame); the Dunlop "Maxply Fort," $30.00 (frame); the Gray's "Light Blue," $26.00 (frame); the Davis "Imperial," $28.00 (frame); the Slazenger "Challenge Championship," $30.00 (frame). In front: Fred Perry shoes, $23.00; wool/nylon socks, $2.50; Stan Smith shoes by Adidas, $28.00; resin bag, $1.25; leather "Tretorns," $32.00; "Copenhagens" by Patrick, $32.00. (Photos by Benjamin Reeve.)

band might be necessary. There is nothing worse than salt water stinging you in the middle of a point.

If you have problems with a leather grip, a resin bag is useful. A bit of resin sprinkled on the leather handle of your racquet makes holding on a good deal easier.

The protective eye and temple guards that have recently been marketed look ridiculous and are of questionable effectiveness. Technique and caution are the best safeguards against injury, and eye guards promote a false sense of immunity which could foster carelessness.

If you wear glasses on the court, plastic lenses are advisable. Always secure your glasses with an elastic strap before you play.

For women, there's a new bra called the Cameo Suspension Bra which is designed for support during sports.

Finally, warm-up suits. Spanking red and white stripes may look dashing, but since most clubs have adequate central heating, warm-up suits are unnecessary. However, if you feel good in one, use it; until you start over-heating, it won't do any harm.

A squash court can look like a geometric nightmare when you come upon it for the first time, but the lines on the floor have very simple functions.

If you've played tennis, you'll see that the floor markings resemble those on one side of the net, and their purpose is much the same. They come into play only in serving, so ignore them for the time being. The same applies to the horizontal line across the middle of the front wall.

GOING ON COURT

The top line on the front wall, the "tell-tale" or "tin" at the bottom of it, the lines on the back wall, and those on the sidewall are boundaries. *After hitting the front wall, the ball remains in play if it is returned to the front wall before hitting the floor more than once—however, provided it remains in bounds, the ball may hit the back and side walls any number of times before returning to the front.*

The ball is out of play if it goes above the top line on the front wall, or the lines on the sidewalls or back wall. If the ball goes into the tell-tale at the bottom of the front wall, it's also out of play. The last player to execute a successful return to the front wall— within bounds and before the ball strikes the floor more than once

—wins the point. The last player to hit the ball before it goes out loses the point, as he or she does if the ball hits the floor at any stage in its progress back to the front wall.

The upper lines and the tell-tale, like the lines and the net in tennis, are simply the framework within which the game is played. The most obvious difference between the two games is that in squash you don't face your opponent and try to hit the ball toward him. Instead, your opponent stands beside you, and your goal is to bounce the ball off the front wall in such a way that he or she will be unable to get to it, or will have to make a difficult shot. This idea will already be familiar to players of handball, paddleball, or other indoor court games, but involves a re-think for tennis players.

Squash is one of those games, like golf, that provides as much entertainment for novices as for tournament winners. Your first time out will be enough to show you what fun it is. But don't expect miracles.

If you're self-conscious at first, arrange to play at an off-peak time when there won't be many people to see you. If there are two of you, try to rally back and forth, rather than challenging each other. Switch sides from time to time. Don't concern yourselves with the back of the court, but play forward of the service line. When you build up some consistency, begin playing to score points, but don't worry about service or strokes. Be careful to watch out for your opponent: squash courts aren't very big.

In brief, the scoring is as follows: a winning score is 15 points; either the server or the receiver can score; service is retained until the servers loses a point; the server alternates sides after each point. (See Appendix for the finer points of tie breakers, service regulations, and so on.)

If you're alone, stand in the middle and hit the ball back to yourself. See how many times you can do it. Hit it in different directions, and at different heights and speeds. Try to predict where the ball will go, then get there to meet it.

Keep your eye on the ball all the way through to the end of your stroke.

Keep your racquet up and ready when you're not using it. Stay on your toes.

Be deliberate in your movements—try to measure your strides.

Be aware of the other person, not just the ball. This will help not only to avoid collisions, but will also enable you to hit the ball away from your opponent.

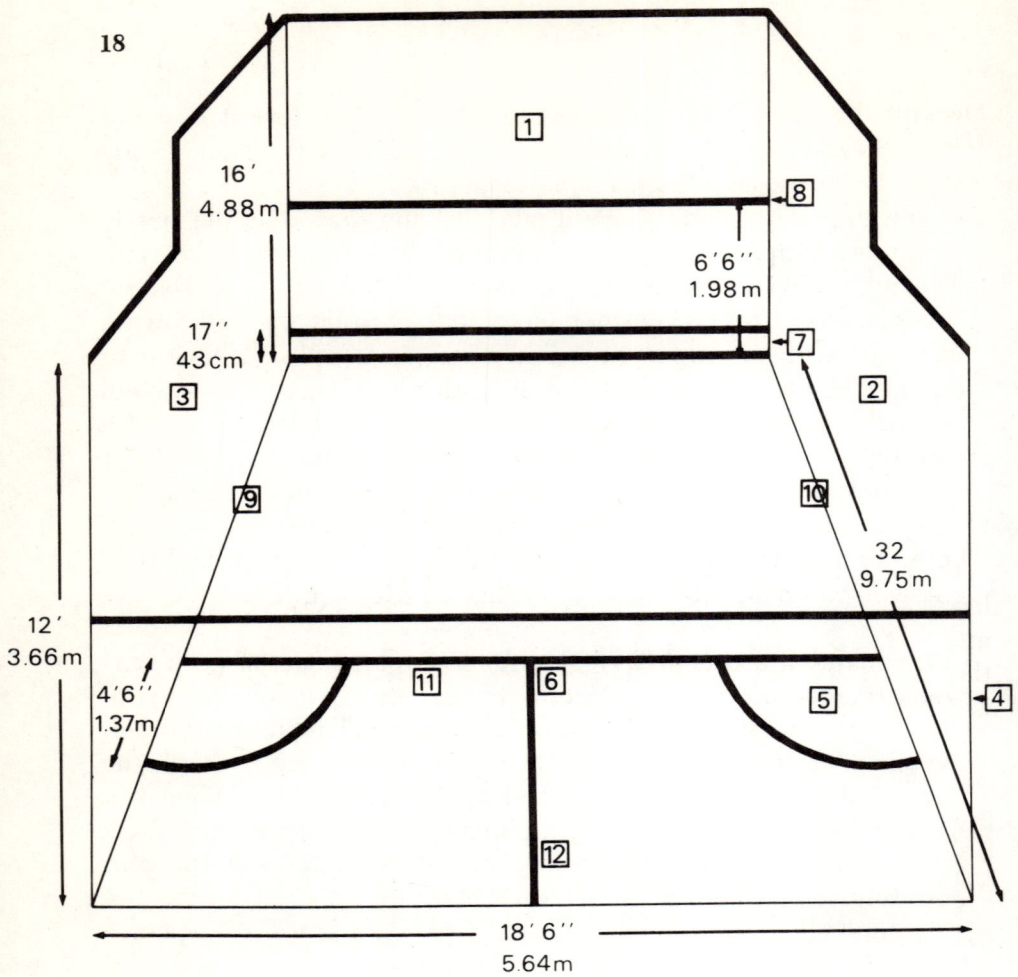

16′ 4.88m	1	8
17″ 43cm	6′6″ 1.98m	7
3		2
9		10
		32 9.75m
12′ 3.66m		
4′6″ 1.37m	11 6	5 4
	12	

18′6″ 5.64m

The layout of a squash court: (1) front wall; (2) right sidewall; (3) left sidewall; (4) back wall; (5) right-hand service box; (6) the "T"; (7) the tell-tale (or "tin"); (8) the service line; (9) the left sidewall nick; (10) the right sidewall nick; (11) the short line; (12) the half court line.

Notice how long your reach is with the racquet fully extended in your hand. You should *always* be at least that far away from the wall: you can still hit balls that pass close to it, and avoid breaking your racquet.

Try to return to the "T," which is the apex of the court, after every shot.

Finally, don't play too long. Squash is vigorous exercise, and it's easy for an enthusiastic beginner to go too far.

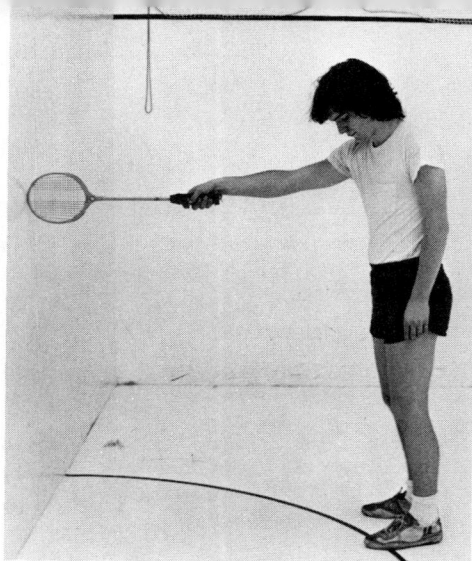

Measuring off from the wall.
(Photo by Benjamin Reeve.)

Once you've played two or three times, you'll have a lot of problems and questions. You should also have begun to establish a mental picture of the court and a sense of the ball's behavior. That's the foundation of your game, and you're ready to build on it. Now is the time to tackle the basic strokes.

Sharif Khan on his toes, ready to go. (North American Open, 1977.)

3

FOREHAND GROUNDSTROKES

Deciding when to play a forehand is no great trick. If you are right-handed, play forehands on all balls that are to the right of the centerline. Running around a backhand in squash is impractical (you'll run straight into a wall, and leave the court open for your opponent), so all balls to the left of the centerline are backhands for a right-hander.

Center all your movements around the "T," which has a much more prominent role than its equivalent in tennis. Squash is all about economy of space and movement, about staying close to the apex of the court, the "T," and sending both the ball and your opponent as far from it as you can.

The forehand is squash's most basic shot. If you are like most beginners, you will instinctively hit it "crosscourt." For example, when you return a ball from the right court onto the front wall, it will bounce—*across the court*—to the left. If you keep hitting cross-

David Linden, of New York, demonstrates the perfectly balanced position for a forehand.

courts, you'll be hitting the ball straight to your partner, and you'll be in trouble.

You should have the entire court at your disposal—and you won't if you hit crosscourts constantly. A crosscourt shot in an enclosed court doesn't go further and further from your opponent, as it does in tennis. Instead, at some point the ball will hit a sidewall and return to the middle of the court. In that case, you concede the "T" you are striving to protect.

The solution is to hit the ball straight into the front wall so that it returns in a line parallel with the right-hand sidewall, and as close to it as possible. Such a shot is called an "alley" or "rail" shot. It exploits the whole court, and when the ball is on the forehand side, it should be the instinctive response. You should have to *decide* to play a crosscourt. (See diagrams pp. 27 and 29.)

When you're learning how to hit a forehand alley shot, start with the swing. You don't need a ball, but a mirror helps, so your bathroom might be a better place than a squash court to start.

Do not grip the racquet too tightly as you will tend to do if you've played tennis. Unless your grip is relaxed, the muscles in your arm will be tight, and you'll have a swing that's frozen from the shoulder and is slow and ungainly. A squash swing is like a golf swing: the muscles in your wrist and elbows must be loose to provide the leverage and snap.

Hold the racquet in a comfortable, handshake grip. Be careful to avoid smothering the index finger with the thumb. If you're not careful, you'll lose a lot of the "feel" of your shots and the thumb will interfere with a smooth swing.

The handshake grip. (Photo by Benjamin Reeve.)

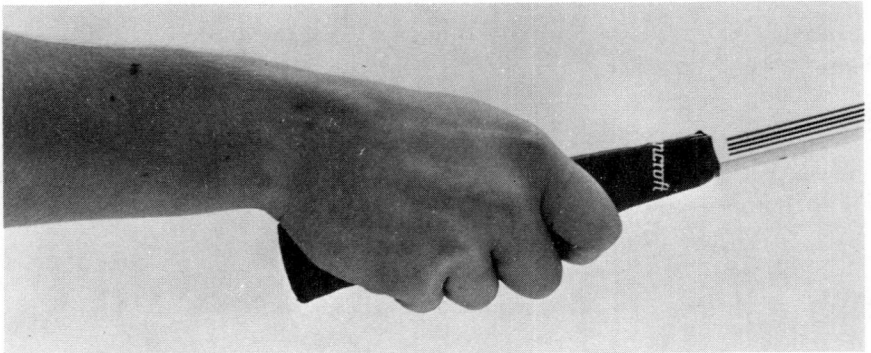

The ball is rising to the top of its bounce, and the leading leg has moved toward it in order to steer the stroke.

With the racquet in your hand, face the right-hand wall of the squash court or the bathroom wall with your feet about shoulder-width apart. Hold your racquet at your feet, at a right angle to the wall. Without changing your grip, or releasing it, turn the racquet so that it is parallel with the wall, and then lift it until it's in a vertical position, strings facing the wall. This is the starting position for the forehand. Your wrist should be cocked, your elbow bent. It's the unwinding of the arm and uncocking of the wrist from this position that will generate the power for your stroke. (See photographs p. 24.)

As the imaginary ball approaches, step toward it. Transfer weight to that leading leg (the left if you're right-handed) and swing your arm to meet the ball. Your knee should be slightly bent.

There are three things to notice in the stroke that will influence the direction of the ball when you come to hit.

First, your leading leg acts as a pointer for your stroke, carrying your racquet along an imaginary line drawn between the toes of your sneakers. For an alley shot, this line would be parallel with or slightly inclined toward the sidewall. As you swing the racquet, straighten your elbow and release your cocked wrist so that it accelerates the racquet through the ball. Without a ball, in the bathroom, this process will be like swatting something just above your left toe.

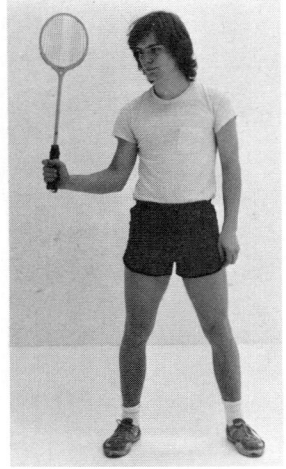

The forehand ready position in three stages. (Photo by Benjamin Reeve.)

Second, keep your head down throughout the stroke so you can watch the ball go right onto your racquet. The key to good contact is always a smooth swing, and your follow-through should carry naturally as far as it wants. When you hit the ball hard, your racquet should finish high over your left shoulder.

Third, try to prevent too much swing in your left shoulder, which will drag the racquet across the line of the ball and make an alley shot impossible.

If you're still in the bathroom now, you shouldn't be.

Forehand alley shots are easy to practice. A properly executed alley shot will at the most only graze the sidewall, so the ball will travel straight back toward you from the front wall—you'll be able to concentrate on your technique without worrying about any tricks the ball might play.

Forehand (and backhand) alley shots are essential weapons in any squash player's arsenal. They never go near the middle, so you keep your opponent away from the "T." They stay close to the wall so that your opponent can't swing solidly at them, and they take the shortest route to the back corners, the worst places on the court. Practice your forehand alley carefully and get into the habit of using it.

One problem that plagues new players, particularly those adept in other sports, is that the forehand seems to offer an opportunity to show their strength. They lean back, heave, and watch proudly

The ball has reached the top of its bounce. As the stroke begins, weight is shifting to the leading leg.

as the ball sails into the gallery. This is the first mistake: trying to hit the ball too hard forsakes accuracy and control.

It is almost impossible to play an alley shot if you generate most of your power from a big turn in the waist and shoulders. Your head will come up as you come round to face the front wall, and the ball can fly anywhere, very much like hooking the ball in golf. If you decide to really clobber the ball, a sense of occasion is apt to overcome all other considerations. Pumping rubber is dangerous to the muscles in your arm, to your racquet if there are walls near, and to your partner, who might not be agile enough to avoid the flailing racquet.

Another problem could be laziness. If you pay insufficient attention to the direction, speed, and trajectory of the ball, you may be making last minute adjustments with your racquet and swing. Your swing should be consistent; move your feet so that it can be. Be prepared to move both forward and back, and side to side. The best place to hit the ball is at the top of its bounce. Before you move your racquet, use your feet to get in position.

You may find the ball passes harmlessly by the stem of your racquet—which seems to have too many holes in it. Practice swings can help. Stand and swing the racquet, observing the head throughout, but particularly at the point where you'd be meeting the ball. After a while, you'll develop a sense of where the racquet head goes

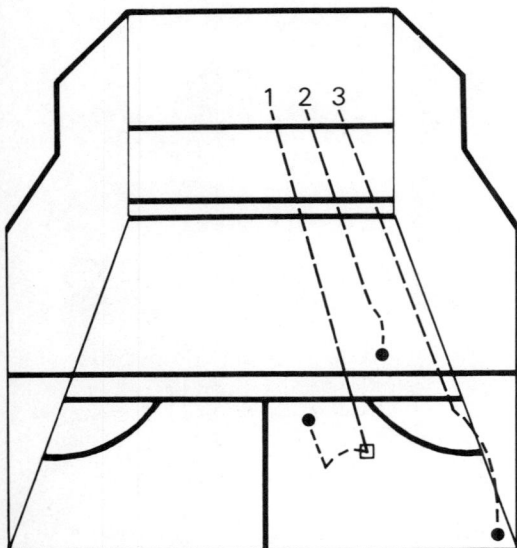

This diagram illustrates the different lengths to which squash shots are hit: (1) long, (2) short, (3) good length.

when you swing, without having to look at it. Pay more attention to the stroke than to where the ball is going afterwards.

It's very easy to play a forehand off the wrong foot. Many advanced players do it when pressed for time, and can still play alley shots accurately, but when you're just starting you'll probably miss the ball completely, or lift it high in the air. Be orthodox, at first, and get your weight onto the left foot.

Hitting the alley shot straight isn't the whole story. If you hit it so hard that it goes all the way to the back wall on the fly, it will bounce back toward the middle, and give your opponent the space to play an easy shot. Playing a ball that comes from behind is very easy, provided you wait for it to come to you and then go chasing after it. A ball like this is "long."

If you hit it so that it bounces in the front half of the court, your opponent will have plenty of space to play the shot. This kind of shot is "short."

A "good length" shot will bounce for the second time close to the back wall. Your opponent will have to hit the ball moving backwards and running out of room if your alley shot or even crosscourt is hit to a good length.

Having emphasized the importance of alley shots, there are a couple of other basic forehands that can be useful: the crosscourt and the short kill.

On the downswing, the elbow has almost straightened, and the wrist is about to be released.

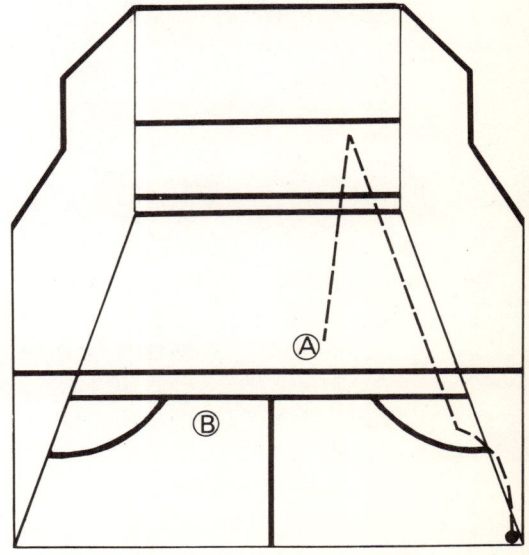

The forehand alley (or "rail") shot: one of the many situations in which it is effective. From the backhand quadrant, player B is not in a good position to return A's forehand alley shot.

Edie Tuckerman prepares to hit a long ball which is coming towards her from the back wall.

The ball is struck as it comes level with the left foot. Weight transference to the leading leg is complete.

The crosscourt can be used to win a rally or to move your opponent from one back corner to the other, but only when he or she is out of position, away from the "T." The technique is easy, this is probably the only squash shot you were born with. Simply open your stance, keep your head down, and swing.

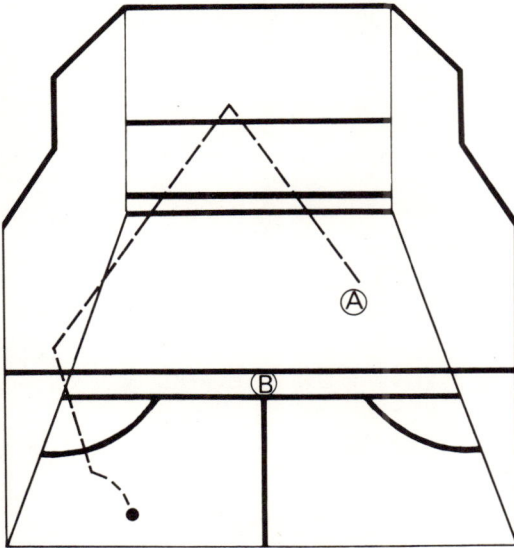

The forehand crosscourt: in this case, player A hits a crosscourt, forcing player B to move from the "T" to the back left corner.

From her position at the "T," Heather McKay should have little trouble with Henri Salaun's crosscourt shot.

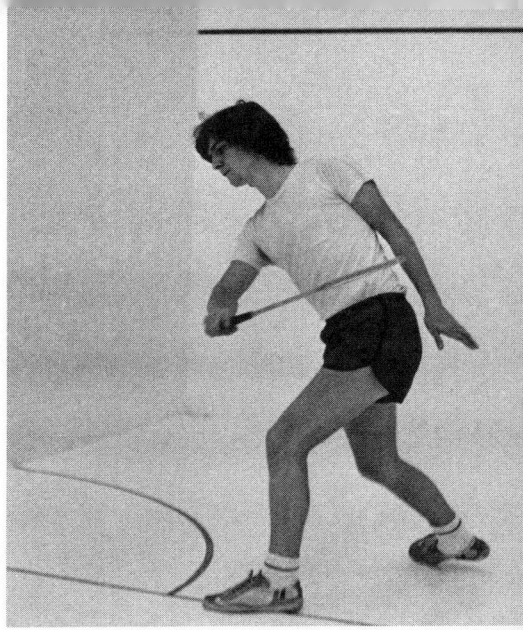

At the beginning of the follow-through, weight remains on the leading leg to prevent hooking, and the racquet arm begins to wind up again.

The short kill is just like an alley shot or a crosscourt, but lower. When you get a weak return from your opponent, hit it hard and low toward either the forehand or the backhand nick (the forehand is easier) and your opponent will have very little chance of

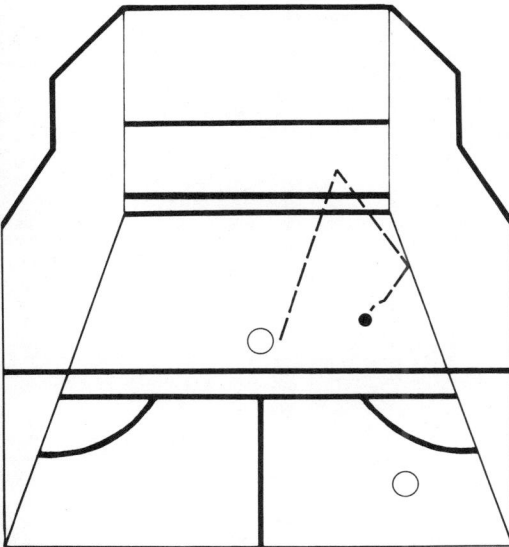

The short kill: with your opponent out of position, hit a low, sharp forehand. The ball should come off the front wall, hit the forehand nick, and roll along the floor.

getting it as it will roll along the floor. A little cut (see "Spin" in "Advanced Techniques") will make the ball die away more quickly. Obviously accuracy is crucial to this shot, so don't try it before you've practiced it or when you're under pressure.

Finally, when you're learning to play these shots, take things slowly and don't just practice. Until you reach advanced levels, you'll always get better by playing rather than by practicing, and too much practice can be deadly dull.

As the stroke is completed, the racquet ends high over the left shoulder.

4

BACKHAND GROUNDSTROKES

The backhand groundstroke—which is, essentially, the mirror image of the forehand—cannot be avoided. If your opponent notices any reluctance in you to play backhands, you're sure to receive as many as can be managed. Once you have a backhand, you will find the "T" is accessible from the left, and squash begins to look like a sensible game. (See "Advanced Techniques.")

There is a theory current among some coaches, and readily endorsed by players whose backhands are poor, that the backhand is necessarily weaker than the forehand. As you read how the basic stroke is made, and watch the flip-throughs, it will become clear that the unwinding motion of the body provides at least as much power as the forehand, although you may find the backhand more difficult to learn.

Start with the swing. Once again in the bathroom, grip the racquet as you did for the forehand. There is no reason to change

Billy Andruss stepping out from the "T" to play his backhand.

your grip for the backhand, as you would playing tennis. There is no time to do so anyway.

Swing a forehand from the top of the backswing, leaning your weight onto the left leg and bending your knee. At the top of the forehand follow-through, stop. Hold the racquet there, and in your mind's eye watch the ball speeding away.

From this position, simply swing the racquet back along the same arc, completing the stroke with the racquet in the position from which you began the forehand. Lean onto your right leg as you swing, bending the knee. That is the backhand swing.

As with the forehand, the moment of contact with the ball is the point when your arm and your racquet are extended almost in a straight line. This should occur when the racquet is slightly in front of the lead leg, as you are shifting your weight onto it. On the forehand, the racquet arm trails, while on the backhand, it leads.

It will take a while to make the forehand and the backhand symmetrical. To speed the process up, swing faster, being careful not to break any medicine bottles. Swing through a loose forehand, stop, lean onto the other leg and swing right back, gradually increasing the rhythm. When you have swished the racquet back and forth for a while, and feel comfortable with the motion, the time has come to take the backhand onto the court.

The end of the forehand follow-through is the starting point for the backhand swing. (Photo by Lawrence A. Armour.)

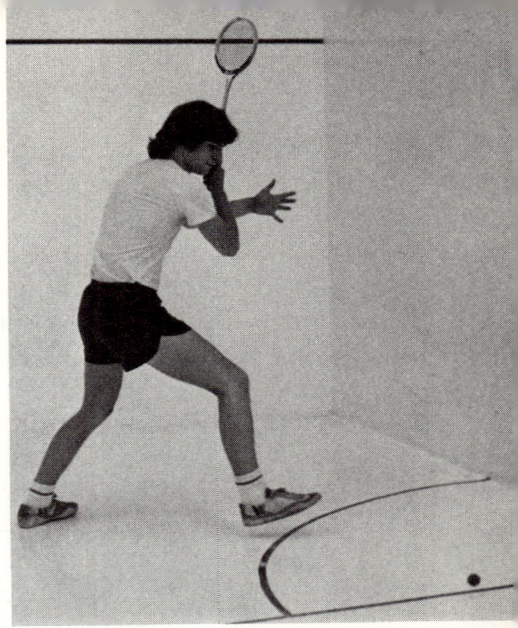

As the ball comes across, the leading leg moves out to meet it.

On the court, the first thing to realize is that, as a right-hander, you should swing the backhand across your left side. Therefore, the body should be inclined toward the left-hand wall. There is no time and no reason to spin all the way around.

When you start practicing with a ball, decide from the beginning where you want it to go. If you're on your own, concentrate not only on hitting it, but on having it come back to you. In other words, learn the backhand alley shot first.

Don't stand flat-footed. Get your feet moving so that you hit the ball from a comfortable position at the top of its bounce.

Use the whole swing. Many people take the racquet down and through in a series of stutters which always confuses things. Try to be smooth.

A few problems may persist that could interrupt your progress to a fluent background groundstroke. At first, no matter how hard you try, you might not be able to make contact with the ball. To rectify this, return to the bathroom, study the flip-through pictures and the text, and swing away. As you do, watch the racquet as it passes the point where you hit the imaginary ball, and keep in mind how far from you that is.

Go back to the court. Stand in a position from which you would hit a ball running straight down the left-hand wall. Be honest, and don't worry about the racquet. If your racquet hits the wall, you are still over-swinging on the backhand, swinging beyond the ball so that it passes between you and the racquet head. You're standing too close to the ball. Because backhands are strange to start with, you want to have the ball as close to you as you can.

Another problem which arises partly from standing too close, and partly from lazy footwork, is an inability to do anything but hit the ball across the court. On the backhand, due to the body's construction, it is impossible to have an open stance (i.e. to stand inclined to the front wall) and have the ball go straight. The racquet always finishes on the right side and will therefore have swung across the body and hit the ball into the right court.

There are two ways this can happen. You might be moving too far and stepping behind the line of the ball with your left leg, then whipping the ball off your knees. If so, you will frequently find yourself out of position in the background court or actually colliding with the backhand wall. (See the section in "Advanced Techniques" concerning movement around the "T.") It could also be that as the ball approaches your backhand, it looks as though it is going to collide with you, and, instead of moving inside, you simply pull the right leg across and out of the way, and swing into the space provided. It's the only way to get good contact if the ball's too near you. You end up with an open stance, weight on the wrong leg, and once again the ball sails into the right-hand court.

The point of contact in a properly executed backhand. (Photo by Lawrence A. Armour.)

The line of the shoulders matches the line between the feet as weight comes down on the leading leg and the swing begins.

Left-hander Peter Briggs winds up for a hard backhand drive against Dave Linden.

Opponent Clive Caldwell looks on as Sharif Khan reaches forward to recover this ball. From this position, Khan's shot will almost inevitably be a lob.

The solution to both problems is to stand parallel to, or even inclined toward the sidewall. Be steady on the right leg when you swing and take great care to be *inside* the line of the ball. Again, the plane of your body at the moment of impact is the most important influence on the direction of the ball.

Another common problem, particularly at the beginning, is that the ball flies high in the air whenever you hit it. This is because you're connecting with it too early. At the best point of impact, just forward of the leading leg, the racquet is almost parallel with the front wall. The ball should fly low and straight. If you swing too quickly, and meet the ball out in front of you, the racquet is on its way up, and the ball will go with it.

You must allow the ball to reach you before hitting it. Once again, it is a question of being relaxed, and using your feet to get in position, then waiting to hit it. Don't just jab at the ball as soon as you see it.

Perhaps the most difficult problem to correct is one that is manifest not only in beginning players but also in intermediates as well. For intermediates it is often the last technical obstacle. Every-

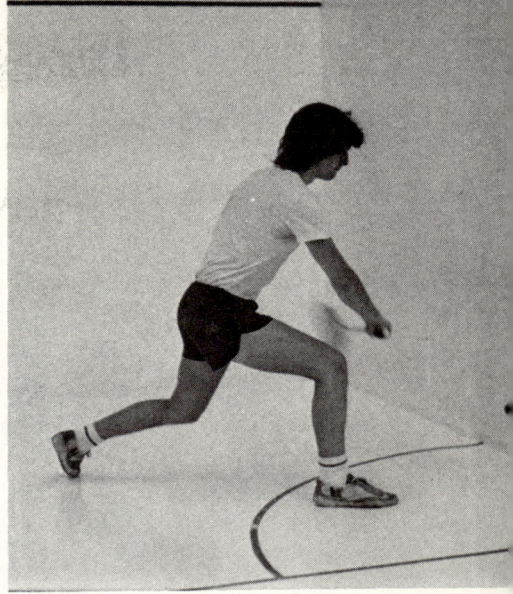

The elbow has straightened and the wrist is about to be released.

thing else is fine: you consistently hit the backhand, and it often goes where it should, but you can't hit it as hard as your forehand. It is a condition that frequently afflicts tennis players who instinctively use hard-won tennis backhands on squash courts. (See "Squash for Tennis Players.")

The first thing to consider is your racquet. If it is too heavy, it will show in your backhand before your forehand. Next, look to your footwork, grip, and court position. Make sure you are releasing your wrist when you swing. If all these factors seem normal, then there is something the matter with your stroke. It is almost invariably this: you meet the ball correctly, just in front of the front leg, with your arm straight, but the speed of the downswing jams your elbow locked, and the straight arm and racquet either stop at the point of impact or swing too wide on the follow-through. The speed of the stroke is impaired as soon as the elbow locks; and the follow-through is inhibited, making recovery for the next stroke slower.

You need the wrist and the elbow as levers in a squash swing. When you try to hit hard with a locked elbow, every muscle in your arm and shoulder will be stretched. If your arm and shoulder ache after squash you probably make this mistake.

Many people grin and bear it, deciding simultaneously that this must be one of squash's tests of character. But there are two simple remedies. First, make sure that you are waiting long enough, in other words, that you aren't reaching forward with the racquet to hit the ball. Your elbow locks as soon as you do. Second, try to remember the compactness of the squash swing. The only point in the entire arc where the racquet and arm are fully extended is at the point of impact. Your arm has unwound from its starting position to get there, and should wind up again on the follow-through.

Two tricks to develop compactness and consequently speed in the backhand swing: very simply, pretend you're either slinging a frisbee or you have a newspaper tucked under your right arm, which you won't let go of as you swing. If that doesn't work, use a real newspaper. The movement encouraged by this exercise is a little exaggerated, as you can see from the flip-throughs, since no newspaper would stay under that armpit. But it will break you of a bad habit.

An ugly, ineffective straight-arm follow-through. Notice that the elbow is locked. (Photo by Lawrence A. Armour.)

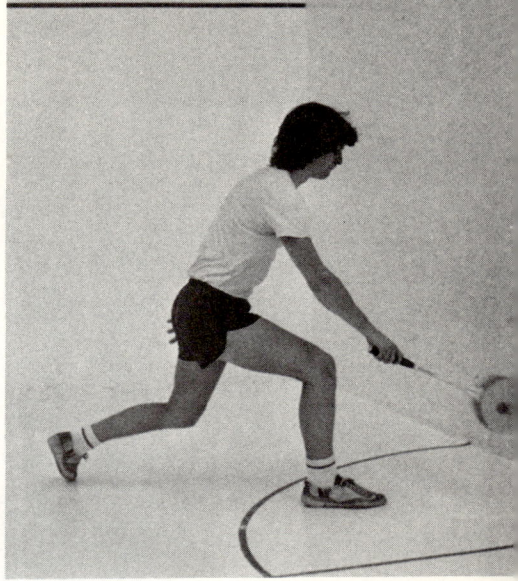

At the point of impact the arm and racquet are fully extended, and weight is firmly on the leading leg.

Moving up the court for a backhand groundstroke. (Photo by Benjamin Reeve.)

Like the forehand, the backhand has three basic variations. The alley shot is the primary one, and should be the instinctive shot. It has much the same function as the forehand equivalent, and is often used to confine someone deep on the backhand side if he or she seems to have a backhand weakness.

Junior champion Alicia McConnell shows off a nice, high backhand follow-through.

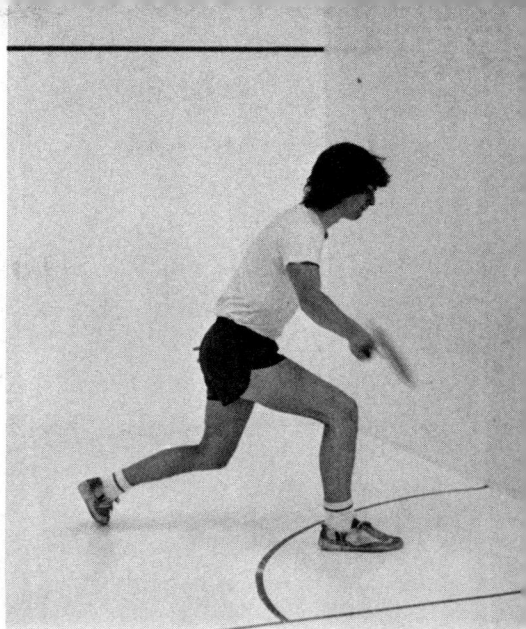

The wrist has gone right through the ball and the elbow is about to wind up in the follow-through.

The backhand crosscourt is usually stronger and easier than the alley shot, and it reverses the usual trend of attack of leading play over to the left side. It is too frequently used by beginners, who feel safer on the forehand side and want to go back over. It may be used effectively from the front, but is most dangerous from deep in the court unless your opponent is also out of position.

As with the forehand, a straight or crosscourt backhand may be hit hard and low with cut toward a nick to win a point at the front of the court.

Once you have a backhand with an alley shot to match your forehand, you have a good deal of the equipment necessary to play squash. The chapters that follow are, for the most part, more complicated variations on the same theme.

Sharif takes one off the back wall in an exhibition match with top U.S. pro Stu Goldstein.

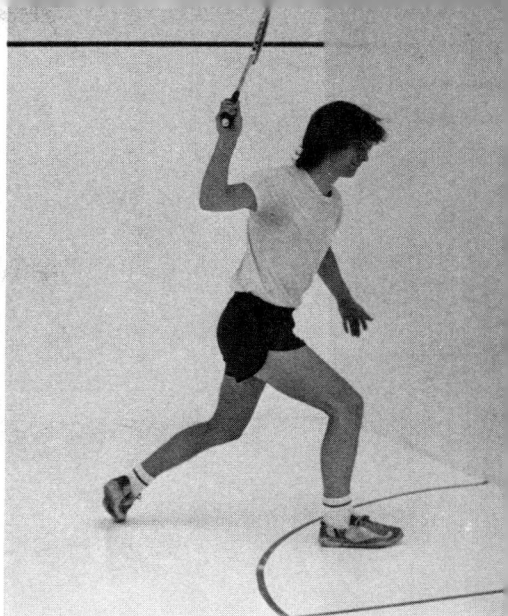

The top of the follow-through.

5

THE SERVE

Serving is squash's third basic skill. Until you can serve well you won't cash in on your first and most obvious source of points.

The serve is the only free shot in squash. Your opponent always receives it in a defensive position, and if you serve well, will stay at a disadvantage throughout the point. The importance of serving is forgotten by many of the better players in the game, who treat it merely as a means of putting the ball into play. When you're beginning the game, the intrinsic advantage in serving is best illustrated. If you make a good serve to another beginner, the odds are that you'll win the point without even receiving a return.

The first serve to learn is the simple lob. Start in the right-hand service box, since you will use this type of serve most often to exploit the right-hander's backhand. Your racquet should make contact with the ball from underneath. Put the ball out in front of you as you swing. Begin with your back leg in the inside front corner of the service box, with your front leg over the service line. You will be within easy reach of the "T" for your next shot.

Holding the racquet high, throw the ball in front of you, and

Steve Vehslage, U.S. champion in 1965, sets for a left court serve.

swing. The high racquet is a good habit, since it will make the lob indistinguishable from other serves until the ball is actually in flight. Your control will be better as well.

When you're learning, concentrate on establishing regular contact with the ball: accuracy comes later. Have a court to yourself to practice. There's nothing worse than publicly failing at something that looks so easy. In a game, having served, move quickly across to the "T" for your opponent's return. Develop the habit as you practice.

The standard left-court serve is the second one to learn. It is frequently used from the right court as well. The mechanics of the stroke resemble those of an ordinary forehand. Stand with your back leg in the service box, and lean toward the "T" on the other one. Instead of lifting the ball, aim to give it speed. Strike it at the optimum point of the swing, when it is beside you, even with the front leg. Hit through the ball this time, rather than swinging in a gentle, upward arc. Make sure the racquet is high and transfer your weight onto the left leg as you swing. When you make contact, you should be close to the middle of the court, and have a very short distance to travel to the "T." A right-hander's return on the forehand is likely to be stronger than on the backhand, so try to cut

The service from left court. Notice how the server should be moving forward and across to the right during delivery. (Photo by Benjamin Reeve.)

Throw the ball gently forward and toward the sidewall. From the low point of the swing, the wrist begins to lift the racquet through the ball.

down the space available to your opponent's return by moving to the "T" as quickly as possible.

There is a third and more advanced serve: the backhand serve, which is usually used from the right court to a right-hander's backhand. Many top players, particularly of the English ball, employ this technique to good effect, but in the lower levels of the North American game it is somewhat neglected. In technique, it is the backhand equivalent of the standard flat serve from left court. It is played with the right leg leaning forward toward the "T."

The backhand serve from right court.
(Photo by Benjamin Reeve.)

For all three serves, there is a different rhythm, and a different "friendly spot" on the wall. When you're familiar with both, the rest will almost happen on its own.

The first, and often the knottiest, problem beginners face is simply hitting the ball. Bear one thing in mind: the arm with the ball is a good deal shorter than the one with the racquet. If you hold the ball at arm's length and swing as you let go of it, it will drop harmlessly to the floor as the racquet head sails by two feet beyond it. To hit the ball on the strings, it must be thrown an arm *and* racquet's length from your body.

Borrow an unstrung racquet from the pro shop at your club. Aim to throw the ball out so that when you swing, it passes through the hole in the racquet head. This obviates some of the tedium of trudging after mis-hit balls, and it's perfectly clear when you're doing things right. The first time you get a serve right will be the last time you miss one.

With the hard serve from left court, players often have problems getting the ball to go where they want it to, usually because of wasted motion. The ball is met as the racquet comes across the body, and is hooked back toward the striker. Slow down and watch your footwork as you deliver the serve. Concentrate on transferring your weight toward your opponent's side of the court.

Many people hear the word "serve," and think of the long, contorted tennis serve. It might be that a good deal of speed and even some penetration can be achieved by adapting a tennis serve to squash, but it is a pure waste of time. In squash, you can do anything with serves from waist height that you could from above your head.

The serve should not only be difficult for your opponent to return but also give you plenty of chance to get across to the "T." If it doesn't, your opponent will have a lot of space to hit the ball into. The serve should be an attacking weapon.

The Lob Serve.   You should almost always choose your opponent's backhand to serve to. The lob serve, as we've said, is the simplest, and it is designed to test the weakest and most taxing stroke in anyone's game, the high overhead backhand.

Hitting the corner is the key to serving successfully, but if you aim directly for it, the ball will pass through far too much open court, and give your opponent a good shot at the ball well before

As the racquet comes up, the body begins to turn.

you're ready. You should aim for a point high up on the backhand sidewall that is even with, or slightly in front of your opponent. The ball will come off the wall and travel across the backhand corner, then bounce before it gets to the back wall. The bounce should prevent it from shooting out of the corner and giving your opponent time and room to deal with it. A serve that hits the back wall is a long serve; a serve that bounces before the back wall is a good length serve; a serve that goes into the sidewall or bounces short of the back wall, is of course, a short serve.

The receiver has three choices of return on a good length serve, none of them easy: play a high overhead before the ball hits the sidewall (if he or she can reach); play the ball in the air as it comes out from the sidewall; or try to deal with the bounce. You'll have time to get to the "T" for any of these.

There are disadvantages to lob serving. First, because you are striking the ball on the extreme edge of the court, it can come out on the backhand side fairly sharply, perhaps giving your opponent room to deal with it, particularly if he or she is quick. Second, there is a considerable premium, at least in advanced competition, on accuracy. The ball is travelling slowly enough that your opponent will have time to set up and really belt a poorly placed serve, especially if it's short. When serving to the forehand, this fact deters most people from using this serve, unless the receiver has an obvious weakness high on the forehand. Third, when lob serving from the right court, your view of your opponent is obscured. You have to turn 180 degrees to catch sight of him. The slowness of the serve makes this easier, but make sure you turn quickly to give yourself some idea of where to go next.

The Hard Serve.   This is most often played from the left court to the receiver's forehand. There are two basic types.

The first is almost a replica of the lob serve, except faster and lower. Aim to hit the sidewall even with or just in front of the receiver, and force him or her into the corner by having the ball bounce before it hits the back wall. Since you're striking the ball toward the middle of the court, it will stay closer to the sidewall on the other side. This hard serve doesn't work as well from the right court, since it is struck from the extreme edge of the court, and will kick out from the sidewall to an even greater extent than the lob serve because of its speed.

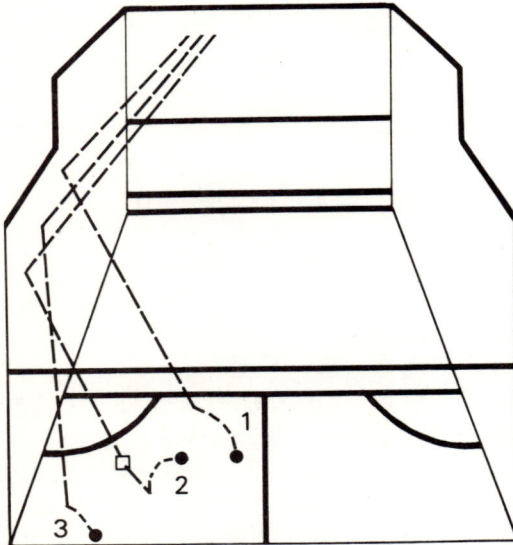

Lob serves to different lengths: (1) short, (2) long, (3) good length.

At the point of impact, the racquet hooks up and across; weight lands firmly on the front leg.

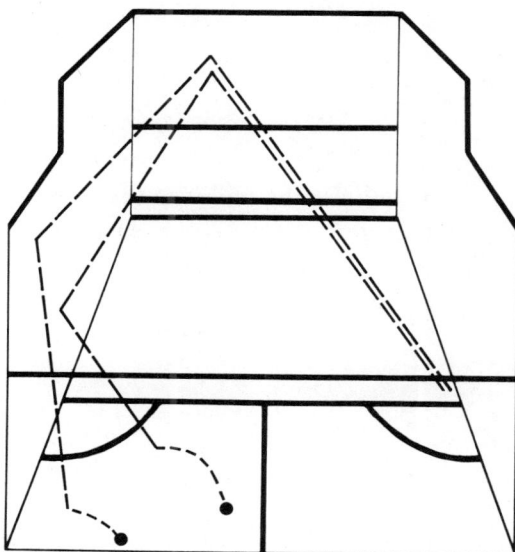

This diagram shows how a hard serve moves out from the left wall at a sharper angle than does the lob serve.

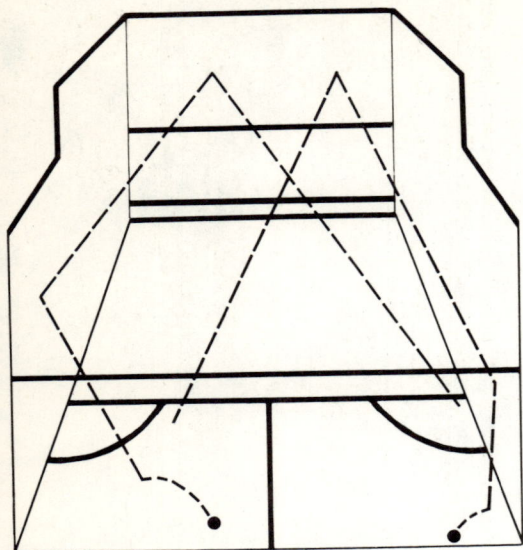

Hard serve: from the left, from the right. Notice that the hard serve stays closer to the sidewall when served into the right court.

The second type of hard serve is effective from both sides of the court. The object is to blast the ball into the sidewall at about the same point but a little higher than before, so that the ball hits the back wall on the fly and shoots out toward the middle. This is essentially a shock weapon, and should be used suddenly and sparingly. It is ineffective with the English ball, which gives up after bouncing off two walls.

The Backhand Serve.   The backhand serve has the same objective from the right court as the milder forehand serve from the left, that is, to penetrate to the corner.

It is probably the best alternative to the forehand lob serve from the right court, with the advantages of a constant view of your opponent and easy access to the "T." It is possible to serve a lob on the backhand from the right court, but the dangers when compared with the advantages lead most people to neglect this course.

The body and the racquet continue to swing across as the ball flies into the opposite court.

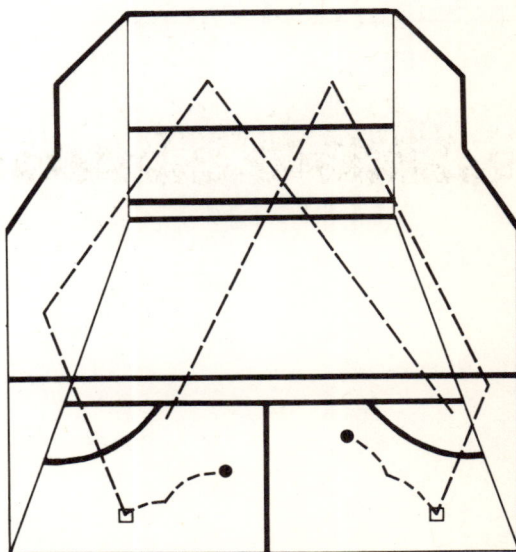

The second type of hard serve should go through from the sidewall and hit the back wall near the floor.

Try to choose your serve in different situations according to your opponent's abilities, not your own predilections. Always serve to weaknesses; you'll make them tell right at the beginning of every point. That can save a lot of labor. And vary your serves. If your opponent grows accustomed to dealing with one kind of serve and one set of angles, throw in something different.

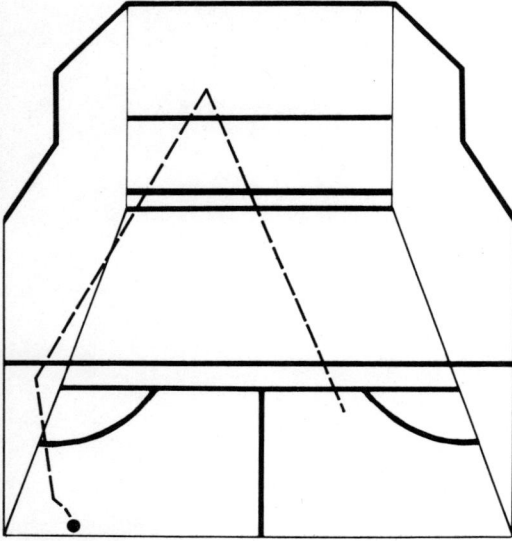

The backhand serve.

The serve is completed. The server should continue to watch the ball and be ready to move across to the "T."

6

FOREHAND VOLLEYS AND OVERHEADS

Volleying, quite simply, means hitting the ball before it bounces. As such, it is a skill required almost as often as groundstroking. If you are to retain control of the "T," you cannot afford to move back in the court to let the ball bounce. Secondly, when in an attacking situation with your opponent out of position, you don't want to allow him to recover. Taking the ball early, while it's still in the air, is one of the principal means of maintaining pressure on your opponent.

Most volleys are played at or around the "T" to preserve the player's position there or to capitalize on it. The forehand volley is an easier stroke once again than its backhand equivalent, and is generally more successfully used.

Everyone has been startled by the power of tennis players' over-

Dave Page sets himself for a smash; Yusaf Khan watches.

head smashes. It is all too easy to transfer the image to squash. The tennis player wants to meet the ball before it gets overhead and out of reach. He or she smashes the ball down and it bounces away from the opponent. In tennis, the smash almost invariably is intended to be winning shot.

A high overhead in squash is quite different. It should be played much less often than the simple volley, as a significant number of high balls will be out of court, and many of the rest will hit the backwall and return at a more convenient height.

However, if the ball is going to bounce before it reaches the back wall (this often requires a fine degree of judgment) and you can reach it, you'd better play an overhead.

Volleys are easier to execute than groundstrokes. You don't have to calculate the bounce, but many of the same rules apply. The ideal point of impact when hitting a forehand volley is about level with the front leg. Your weight should be transferred to this left leg as the shot is made. The moment the arm and the racquet are fully extended is the optimum point of impact.

The most important new factor in volleying is the reduced time available for the shot. A ball travelling through the air goes faster than one that bounces. In an attacking situation around the "T," carrying your racquet high improves your chances of being ready. Up to about shoulder height, there is often a clear choice between aiming low for a kill, which is practical when the ball is below eye level, or playing a safer defensive shot to the back of the court. Your decision should be determined by both the time available to wind up for the shot and your distance from the ball. The racquet work for each type of stroke is different.

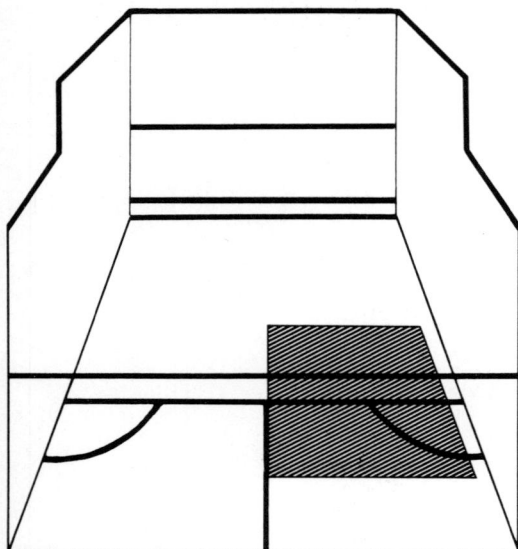

A forehand smash might be necessary within the shaded area.

The racquet goes back as weight moves forward onto the front leg.

Sharif steps across from the "T" to cut off Niederhoffer's long alley shot before it can get through to the back.

Even when the ball is at a manageable height, it is more difficult to aim low and hard. To be effective, you must be very accurate. So, start with the easier, defensive type of volley. In the middle of the court hit the ball slowly off the front wall into the air. Your object is to return the ball to the front wall at about the same height as it first hit. As it comes back again, try to repeat the same thing. Measure your performance by the number of times you can do this. Bear in mind you are learning a controlled stroke, with a short, controlled swing, which punches the ball without elaborate wrist action. By hitting forehand volleys in the middle of the court, you'll learn to control them from the start. Remember that you are catching the ball as it drops and pushing it back up, not hitting through or down on it. As you become more confident at this exercise, move steadily back in the court and closer to the forehand sidewall.

The overhead is a defensive, positional shot. You don't have to hit the ball down over a net as do tennis players. Having established a rhythm hitting lower volleys, feed yourself a few overheads. Again, try to maintain control and a short enough swing that you can repeat the shot. Avoid finishing with your racquet low and your body bent forward—you'll drag the ball down with you.

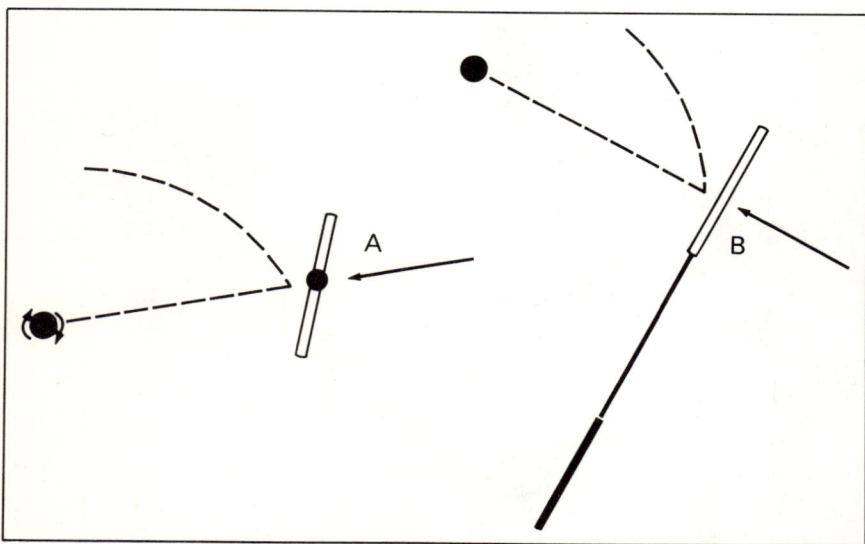

A represents the trajectory and racquet angle for an attacking volley; B represents the defensive volley.

In its lowest position as the ball comes level, the racquet can move up to meet it.

In a match with Frank Satterthwaite, a top U.S. pro, Heather McKay is about to play a low volley with cut to win a point.

SQUASH!   65

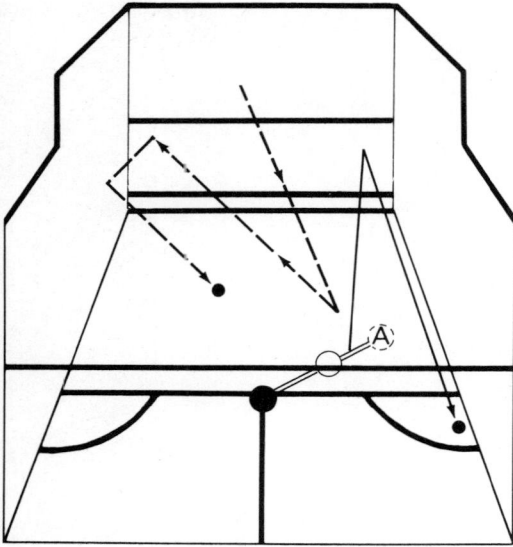

Played correctly, this volley should have landed in the back forehand quadrant (see solid line). Instead, the player ran beyond the line of the ball to point "A." The resulting shot (see dotted line) is a much weaker return.

Only when you can hit both types of unambitious volleys consistently should you begin to experiment with volley kills. The only key to success with these is persistent practice. The margin for error is small, as there is rarely enough time to consciously aim the shot. When aiming low with any volley remember that a little cut will bring the ball down, but too much will make you slow and inaccurate.

The most aggravating difficulty you can have is missing the ball or hitting off the wood into the floor.

The probable reason for either error is panic that the ball is in the air at all; it suddenly seems more elusive. The consequent impulse is to have the whole business over with before anyone sees. This usually means that you swat at the ball before the proper time, very often with eyes closed. If you stand in the flight path of the ball, then miss, it will hit you.

The first step is to overcome this flinching. Don't defend yourself, but be aggressive. If you swat at a ball before it reaches you, your racquet will be travelling downwards when you meet the ball, and you'll either miss or hit it into the floor. Step inside the ball, watch it as though it's a predictable enemy, and meet it at arm and racquet's length when it is even with you.

There are two more difficulties that might occur right at the beginning. The first has to do with footwork.

If you are still on the move when you play a volley, the problem

The racquet at the point of meeting the
ball beside the front leg.

of judging the ball is complicated. You will tend to pull all your
shots into the middle. Make sure your feet are firmly planted and
your head still when you swing.

There may also be a problem incorporating the racquet's length
into your judgment of the shot. Take your racquet and a ball, and
bounce the ball higher and higher into the air. When you can do
this consistently, you can play a volley—you're already using all
the skills required.

As you progress, you may find yourself unable to hit a straight
forehand volley. There are three possible reasons for that: you may
be trying to hit the ball too hard and too early, slogging across
in front of you; your stance could be too open, or, you may be
trying to get back to the "T" before you've finished your shot.

There are, logically enough, three simple answers: wait a little
longer; slow down the rhythm slightly—just take your time; consciously move to the ball from the "T" rather than sidling across
behind it. There is much more unorthodox footwork in forehand
volleying, particularly under pressure, than in any other shot, but
if things aren't working try the orthodox way for a while.

Volleying is the heart of the attack. Your opponent has a minimum
of time to observe and respond. Even in defense, the volley is the
shot that puts pressure on your opponent.

There are three basic situations in which the forehand volley is played. The first is to cut off your opponent's alley shot or cross-court pass, either aggressively or defensively. The interception is usually made from the "T," often at full stretch. It resembles holding the net at tennis.

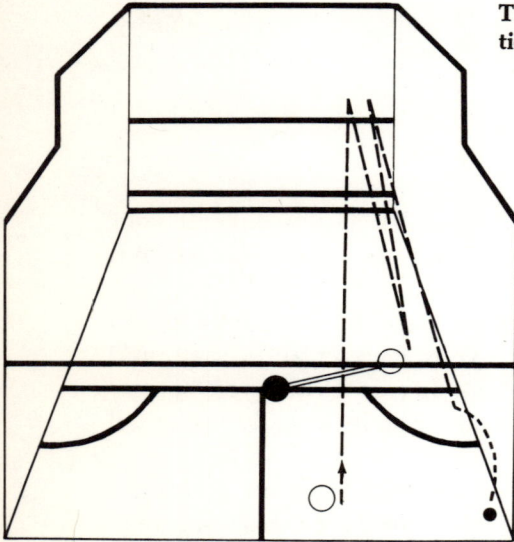

The first application of the volley: interception from the "T."

The second situation is when returning serve. The object then will usually be to obtain access to the "T" and force the server back. The basic service return, then, will be along the right-hand wall to the back. Practice this shot until you can play it with your eyes shut. You'll be off to a bad start every time your opponent serves from the left if you don't get this right. If you do, it will immediately negate the server's advantage. When the server is over-anticipating the volley, the crosscourt return should be played.

After the point of impact, the racquet continues on up and through the ball.

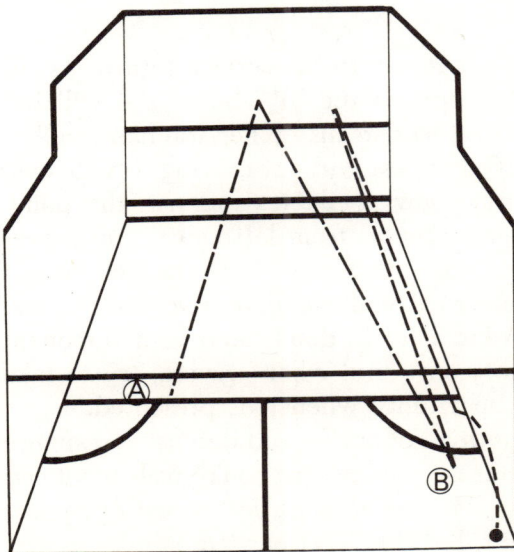

The classic service return of A's serve from left court.

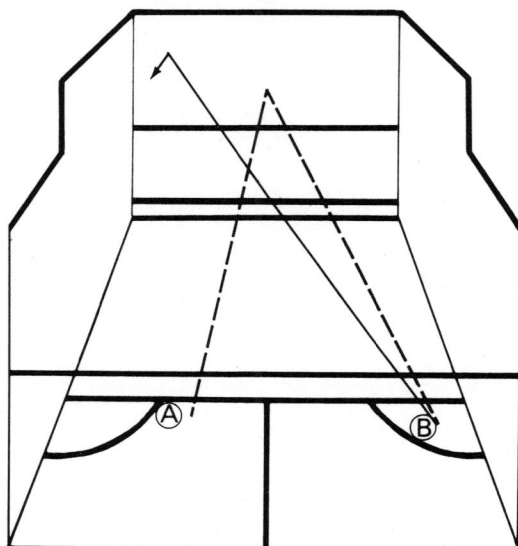

A dangerous service return. If B's return clears
A as he moves to the "T," fine. If it doesn't, A
has an easy job of winning the point.

The third use of the volley is to return the service return. As the
server moves from the right court to the "T," he or she will frequently encounter ill-judged returns to his or her forehand volley.
Since such a ball can be played almost without moving, it behooves
the striker to take all the time now available, and win the point.
On the other hand, if the server serves from left court, and moves
across to the forehand for a straight return, he'll do well to get
across in front of the receiver to make a defensive volley, and
keep him back. When returning a serve, don't hand your opponent
an easy volley by hitting crosscourt, and when serving, try to take
full advantage of such an opportunity when it is presented.

In these basic situations, both an offensive and defensive response
is acceptable. If it is to be offensive, make sure you're well practiced
because if you miss, you lose. Most of the cut and thrust of squash
is in volleying. Don't miss out, but don't get carried away.

Halfway through the follow-through, the racquet is still high; weight should still be on the front leg; and you should still be watching the ball.

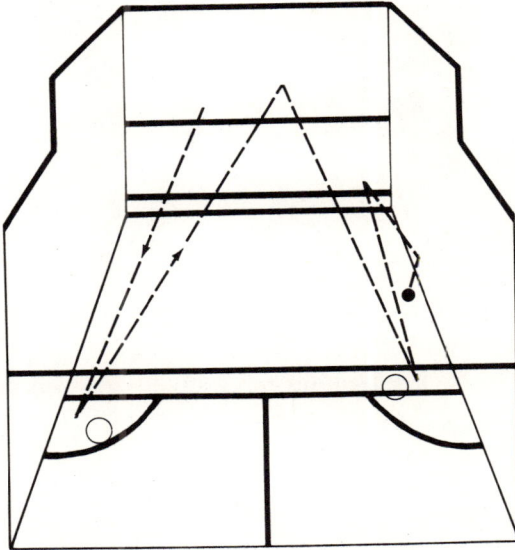

Forehand volley kill of service return.

With her wrist bent far back, Eileen Rubin is ready to cut down on this easy volley.

The top of the follow-through, which will vary according to the power of the stroke.

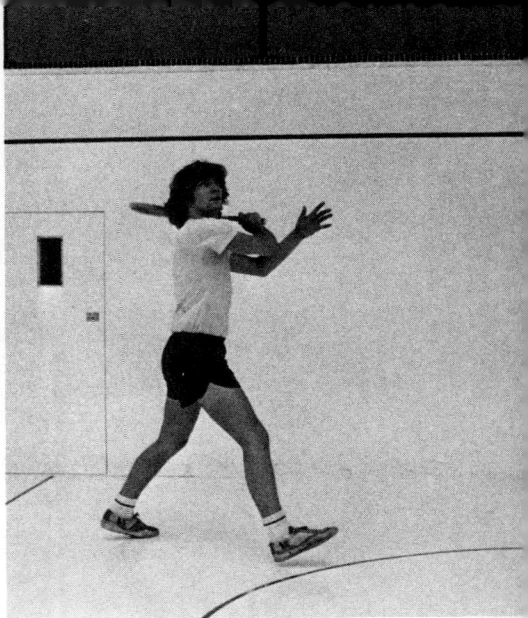

7

BACKHAND VOLLEYS AND OVERHEADS

The backhand volley is the most difficult stroke to master in the early stages of learning the game. Weakness in this department can crucially handicap a player, as it is easy to exploit and is usually the first flaw to reveal itself. But when the shot is played well, it is about the most significant attacking weapon.

As with groundstroke, the main problem is the footwork. Correctness in preparation and an understanding of the physics of the stroke are essential for dealing properly with this.

As on the forehand, the probability of hitting a backhand volley winner decreases as the ball rises above shoulder height. The shot above shoulder height should be a positional one, and this is the kind you should begin with. Squash is a game won on mistakes rather than unplayable winners.

With Mateer at the "T," Bostwick plays a defensive volley to try and escape from the corner.

When you go on court, be conscious at all times of the plane of your body and your footwork. On the backhand, your racquet can't help but move along the line selected by your feet.

Start by teeing up a backhand volley off the front wall. As on the forehand side, try to hit it back on the same side so you can hit it again, and establish a rhythm. At this stage, be content with hitting low, easy balls. This will mean hitting from below the ball with the face of the racquet open, back up to the same height. Think of it as playing catch with yourself off a wall.

On the backhand side, because the racquet arm is in front, aim to meet the ball a little forward of the front leg as you lean onto it. Do not curtail the follow-through unduly, but keep the swing short and precise.

In a properly controlled backhand volley, the racquet should come through from under the ball. (Photo by Lawrence A. Armour.)

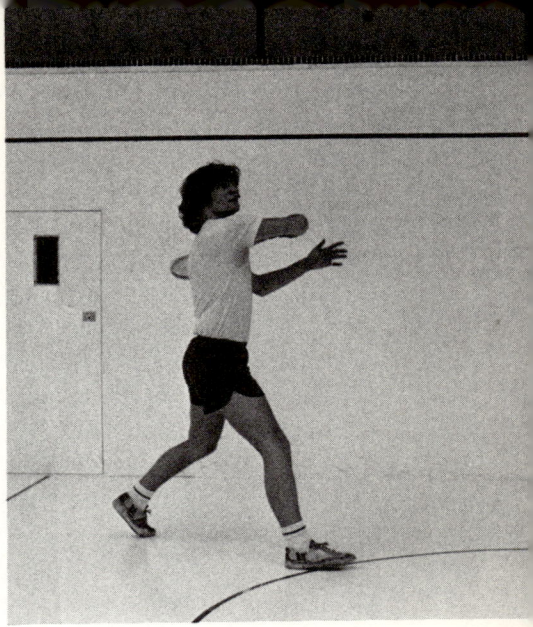

The racquet at its lowest point as weight is transferred to the leading leg.

You will soon notice that one of the main problems with backhand volleying is supplying leverage to the racquet. If you employ the body swing inherent to forehand strokes, you'll hit across the ball. The leverage should instead be supplied in the manner of karate. The left arm comes across in front of the body as the right goes up in the backswing. As the stroke is played, both arms are

As described above, both arms supply leverage at the moment of contact on a hard backhand volley. (Photo by Lawrence A. Armour.)

vigorously returned to their normal positions, and power is delivered by the shoulders springing open. At a high level, some players stamp petulantly as they do this. Don't begin by trying to hit the ball hard in this way, just realize the means employed.

Having mastered low balls, feed some higher. Be most careful at what point in the swing you contact the ball. It is very easy to flip the racquet with the wrist over the top of the ball, and hit it into the floor. This is the reason that hard-hit backhand overheads, which inevitably involve wrist action, are so hazardous.

Only when you've established a good, steady rhythm both low and high, should you begin experimenting with hitting the ball hard. Try the karate-type movement without a ball until it's regular, then take it on the court. It will soon become apparent that as you apply more force, your accuracy and control decrease. To retain accuracy when hitting hard, the body has to be turned a long way toward the sidewall.

This turning away restricts the player's view of his opponent, and takes him further from the "T." Therefore, strive not so much for speed as for accuracy. Remember, a little cut will bring the ball down quickly; but introduce it gradually. Don't try winners from behind the "T" until you're desperate. The stroke is difficult enough from any position—to miss it deep in the court is the classic error.

The problem of missing the ball entirely on the backhand volley is very similar to the same lapse on the forehand. (See Chapter VI for solution.) However, there are a few specific problems with the backhand. They are usually connected with the uncertainty involved in playing "on the wrong side," which will lead to standing too close, hitting too early, or continuing to move the head and feet while hitting the ball. These problems can usually be cured by steady, well-advised practice. (See "Drills.")

A couple of other problems could come up. The first is the elbow-lock, which is made more difficult by the fact that the grip is naturally tighter for volleys, and the arm tends to be more rigid.

Remember that the backhand pivots around the elbow, and that in the short follow-through for the volley, the force of the shot is dissipated by releasing it. Also, if your elbow is locking you may be reaching too far forward for the ball. Just wait a fraction of a second longer, being careful not to finish with the racquet low.

There could also be a difficulty at the beginning with the arc of the swing. Some beginners try to get too far underneath the ball, and the resulting contortions twist the arm and twang the elbow.

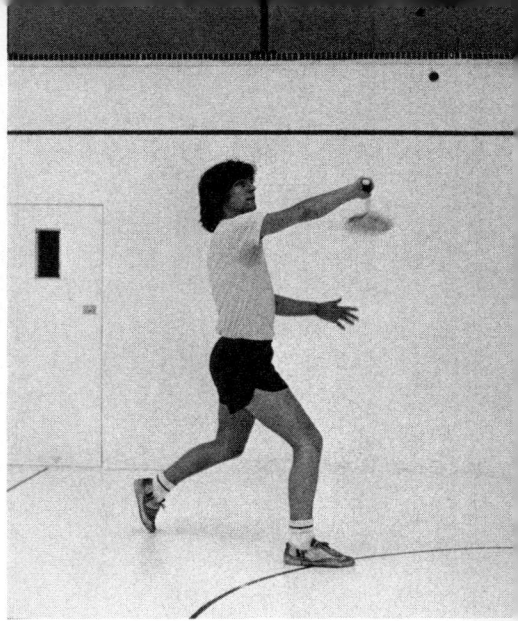

Halfway through the upswing, the elbow has straightened and the racquet is in position to catch the ball as it drops.

In this close-up, notice the footwork on the backhand volley. The alley shot is only possible with the back leg at position "1." The crosscourt is inevitable from position "2."

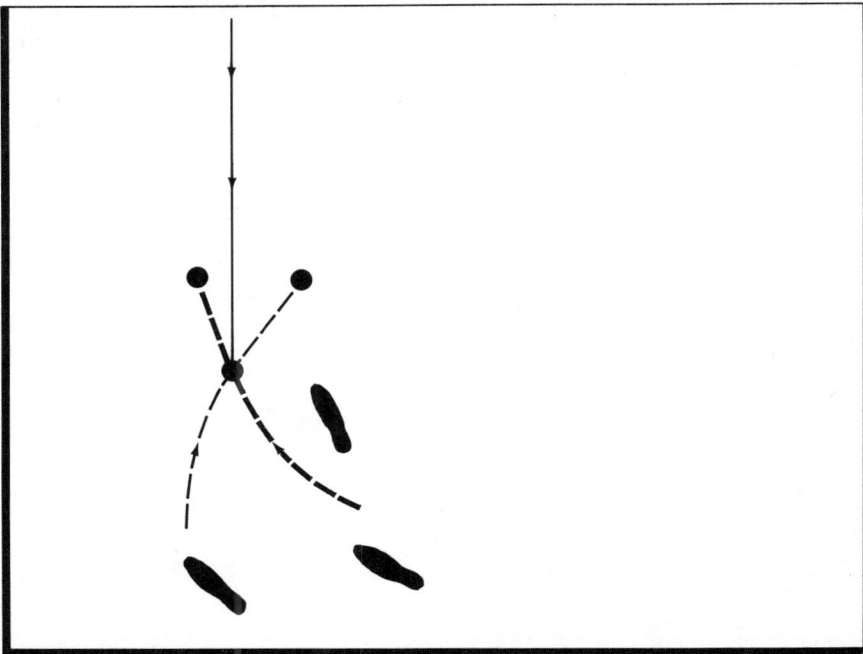

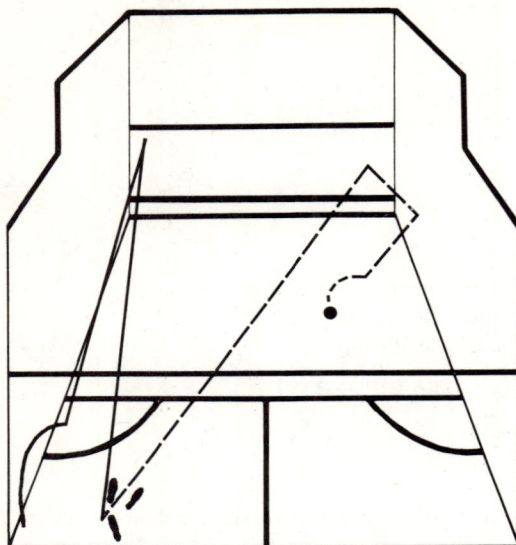

On the backhand volley, the ball will inevitably follow the line between your feet, so your stance will have to be closed if you expect to hit the ball straight. (Solid line indicates the correct position.)

The solution is simple: just swing the racquet back up the arc of the ball you just received.

The second difficulty comes to those persuaded of the boisterousness of squash, those players who think someone's measuring their reflexes. Saving time is the key, so across goes the left leg, swish goes the racquet, and away goes the ball, off into the forehand court as the striker strikes out for the "T" with his head down.

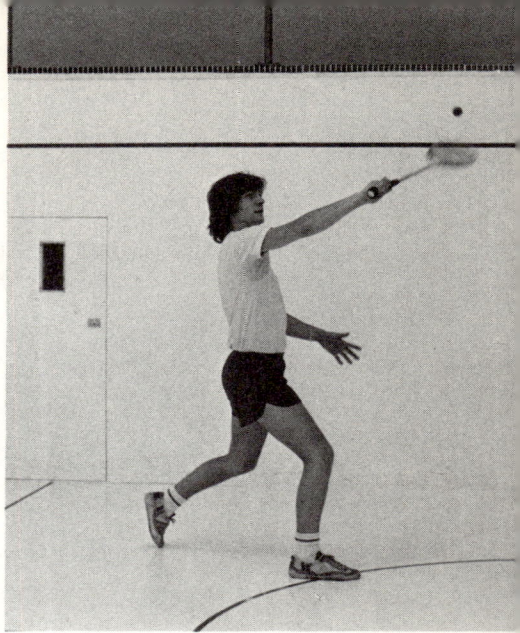

The wrist is straightened and weight comes firmly onto the leading leg.

A. C. Hubbard, a left-hander, plays a straight defensive volley during a doubles match.

Dave Sawyer demonstrates a controlled follow-through as he volleys high to the back against Jim Gorham at the "T."

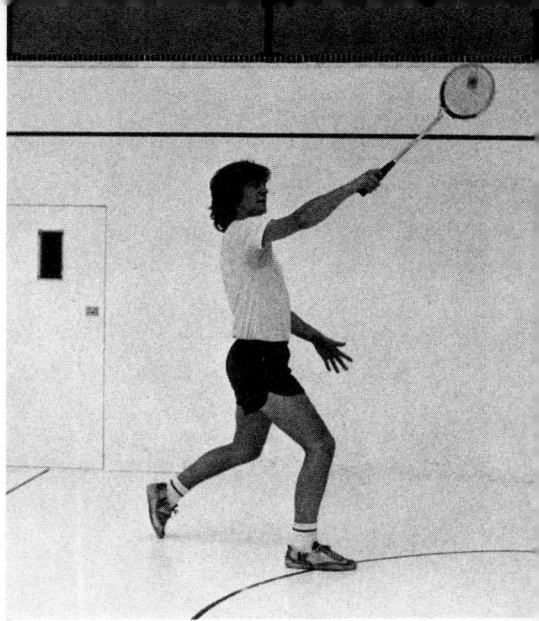

The racquet and arm are fully extended
at the moment of impact.

It is essential to be methodical with this shot. You can't afford to
slug away at backhands in the air, even if you're coordinated
enough to hit them all, they'll wind up in the forehand court, and
your opponent will never have to play a backhand. He might not
like backhands but you'll never find out. Proficiency in the straight
backhand volley is, first of all, the only way to test your opponent's
backhand, and secondly, the only really effective way to return the
dangerous high right-court serve.

Take it slowly: the shot you're playing is probably the quickest
way of winning or losing. Make sure that you're moving across from
the "T" with your right leg forward. Remember, if you play the
shot well, you'll have plenty of time to move back to the "T." Move
smoothly. Unless the ball is up to be killed, cut out all sudden
rushes.

The uses of the backhand volley are more or less the same as for
the forehand: returning serve, cutting off passing shots, and returning the return. However, they have somewhat more importance.
Backhand volleying is more difficult than forehand, and weaknesses
will be found out sooner and are more likely to be serious. On the
other hand, if you're good at the backhand volley, then you have a
most valuable asset, especially if your opponent's is not so good.

If you cut off the pass down the wall, you force your opponent to

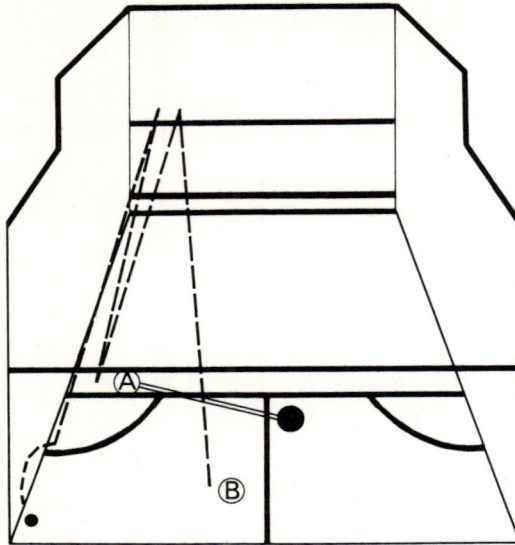

Cutting off passes from the "T." A will prevent
B's attempt to take over the "T."

play another deep backhand; if it's a crosscourt ball you've returned,
your opponent will have a long trip to pick up your ball.

Returning serve on the backhand is a crucially important skill.
Your opponent will be looking for his or her points principally when
serving from the right court. If you can consistently return the serve
down the left wall to the back, then get to the "T," you've removed
your opponent's easiest source of points. Only when your opponent
is chasing over to the left wall even before you've made your return
should you risk a crosscourt volley return. If you do it sooner, you
run the risk of a set up for the forehand volley winner discussed in
the previous chapter.

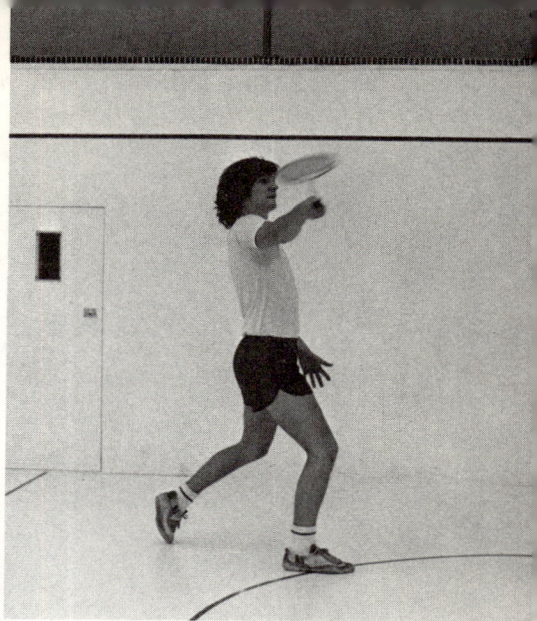

The wrist goes through and the racquet stays high as the follow-through begins.

Returning the crosscourt return with a backhand volley should be almost as easy as on the forehand. The whole court, once again, will be open to you, but the simplest, most obvious way of ending the point is the best. When someone's made it easy for you, why try and complicate things again? Outright winners can be made in all the above situations, but pick your ball carefully. If you make many mistakes, your opponent will put this difficult stroke under immediate pressure.

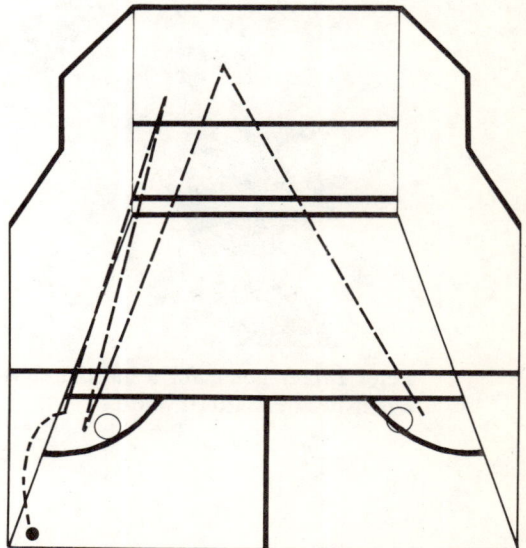

The only safe way of returning serve from right court.

Peter Briggs going for a backhand volley winner with a lot of cut in a match against Frank Satterthwaite.

Weight remains on the leading leg as the stroke is completed.

8

BOASTING: GETTING THE BALL OUT OF THE CORNERS

Anyone who has played squash knows the feeling of impotence which descends as soon as the ball deflects off the sidewall toward that treacherous zone in the rear. Many people grasp the racquet with both hands and awkwardly try to flip the ball out. If this is successful, the ball returns to the front wall and meekly stands up to be killed.

There is a better way, a stroke that can be played on both sides of the court, not only in defensive situations from the back corners, but also further up the court to win points. When those uninitiated see this stroke played out of the back, it looks like magic, though it really isn't. It bears no resemblance to anything

Heather McKay demonstrates perfect form as she steps back to return Frank Satterthwaite's drive with a boast.

89

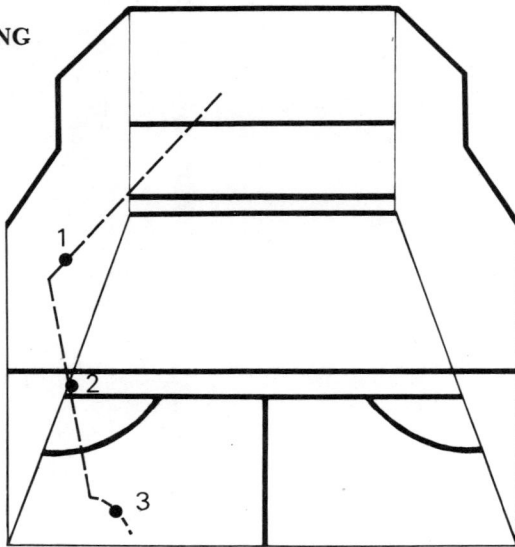

You can return a good length serve from one of these three positions. Position "2" is usually best.

in any other game, but the more you watch, it, the clearer things become.

Boasting adds a whole new dimension to squash. After learning this shot and appreciating its uses, you'll find that squash loses its simple front-to-back and side-to-side character, and reveals the subtleties that make it such an absorbing game. When you first experience the feeling of successfully aiming a ball out of the corners, or

Foot position for the alley return in the air as the ball comes off the sidewall from a good service. Notice that there is enough space between the sidewall and the back wall for a complete swing.

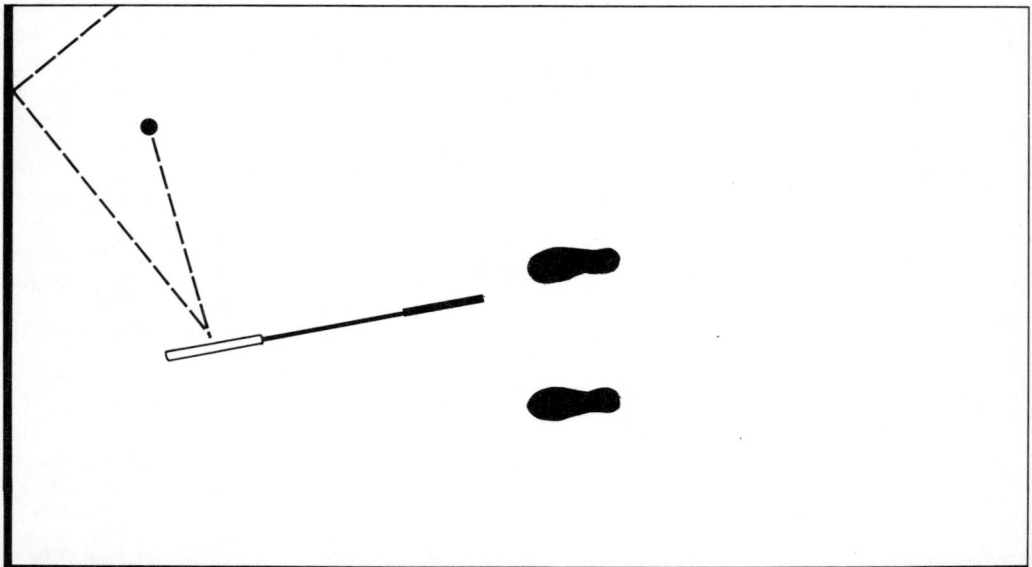

The ball has penetrated to the rear backhand corner and is moving across from the sidewall to the back wall. The player's first move is back toward the corner from the "T." Then the leading leg comes down, still well short of the back wall.

winning a point with a boast, you'll know what I mean.

The best way to begin is to find someone who can play the shot, and watch him or her play it. The next step is to try a few easy ones in the middle of the court, the kind you'll use to win a point, first on the forehand. The preparation for the stroke is the same as for an ordinary forehand. Tee yourself up an easy one, pick the racquet up high, and wait for the ball to come back. Aim the ball *into the sidewall,* have it bounce off and hit the front wall above the tin, and come off again and bounce low in the front left corner, preferably close to the backhand nick.

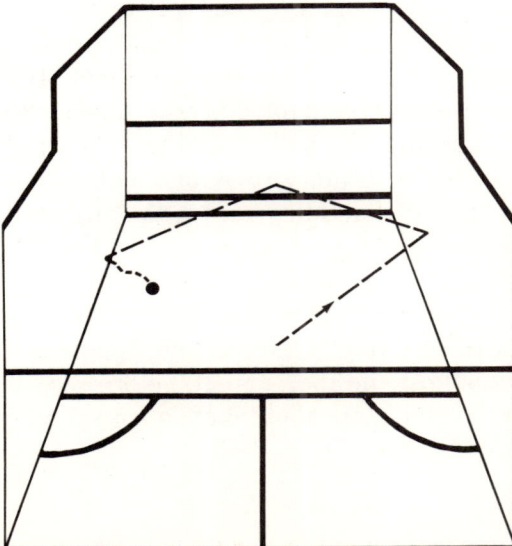

The forehand boast from mid-court, crossing and hitting the nick on the backhand side.

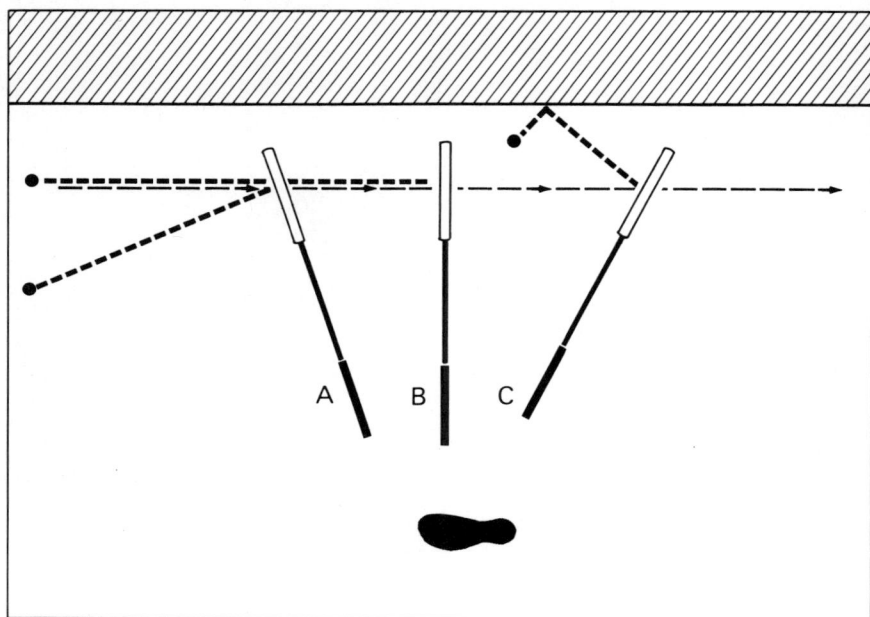

Position of the racquet in relation to the leading leg for: (a) crosscourt; (b) alley shot; (c) boast.

You should be hitting the ball later than on an ordinary forehand when it is already behind your front leg. To play this shot successfully, you need enough room to swing freely. Your left leg has to come across a little further as you play the stroke so that the line to be taken by the ball matches the line between your feet. It'll take you a while to work out the angles involved, how sharply to hit the ball into the sidewall, etc. But the ball should always wind up all the way over in the opposite front corner, and not career back from the opposite wall into the middle. Your attacking shot will be next to useless unless you move your opponent off the "T" to retrieve it.

The opportunities for deception with this shot are endless. As you go to your right to meet the ball, you'll obscure your opponent's view of the ball. Until you actually swing the racquet, he or she will have no idea whether you're playing an alley shot, a crosscourt,

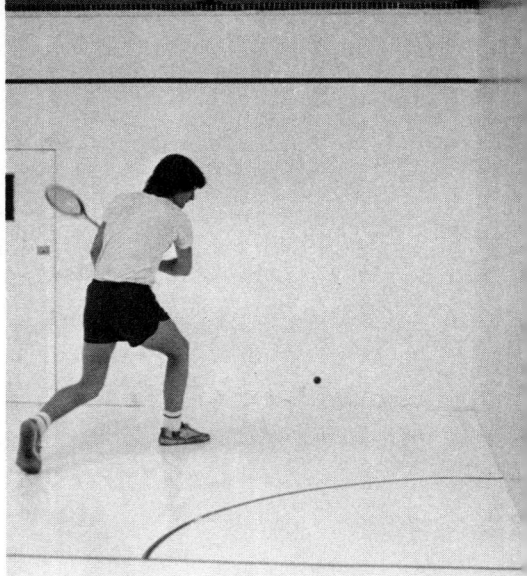

Weight is firmly placed on the leading leg as the ball rises to the top of its bounce and the swing begins.

The attacking boast: as you step from the "T" into the forehand court, your feet should line up in the direction that the ball will travel. (Photo by Lawrence A. Armour.)

or a boast. To maximize the effectiveness of this ploy, do not go in with your racquet flailing, but delay your shot until the last possible second to give your opponent the least possible time to react. A slower shot accomplishes this better than a faster one. The attacking boast can be most effective as a "touch" shot.

The backhand boast requires the same preparation as an ordinary backhand (make sure you're proficient at the latter before you try these).

The attacking boast has many applications, but one classic scenario ensues when you've driven your opponent deep. He or she makes a weak, inaccurate alley shot from behind you, and moves cautiously up the court. You then take the ball in front of him or her, hit it across and into the sidewall where it dies in the opposite front corner almost as far away from your opponent as it could be. This is one of the most common and satisfactory uses for the shot, and is quite often played as a volley with exactly the same principles.

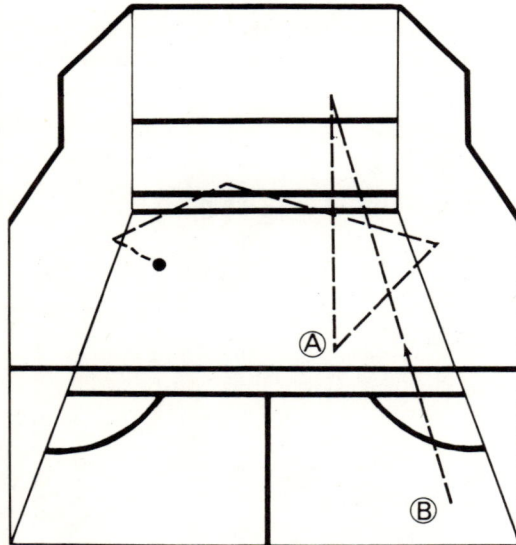

After B's weak shot from the back corner, A can hit a boast across B into the wall so that the ball dies in the opposite front corner.

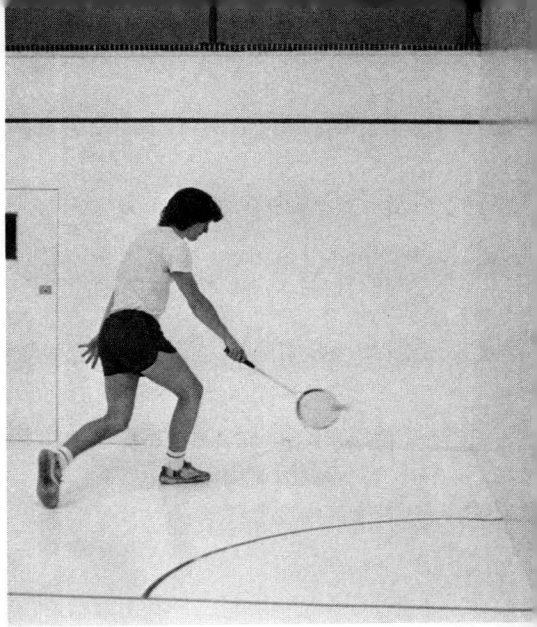

The ball is met well in front of the line
of the leading leg and hit with a hooking
motion.

Another ploy is the corner shot, played as a short kill. Hit the
ball gently toward the front corner. It doesn't matter whether it
hits the front wall or the sidewall first. Hit it low, and your opponent,
racing forward, won't know which way the ball is going until it's
gone.

A third application of the attacking boast comes when a ball is
bouncing out of a front corner and crossing into the opposite court.
If the ball comes out of the backhand corner, for instance, stay

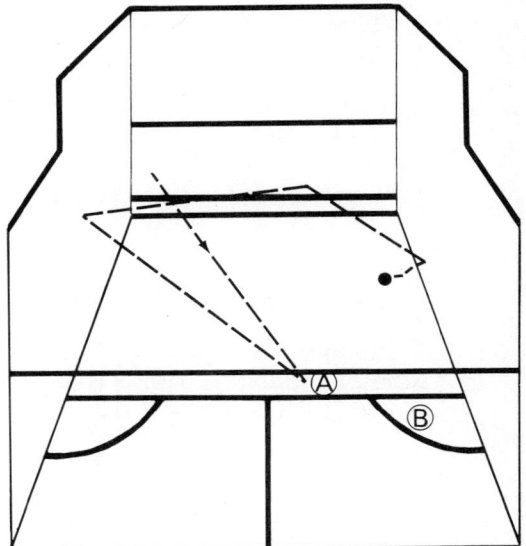

Instead of taking the ball earlier and switch-
ing to the forehand, player A has delayed his
shot and boxed B in so that whether he plays
a boast or any other shot, he's likely to win
the point.

As the ball bounces out of the front backhand corner, Tom Poor backs across the forehand court to box in his opponent, Roger Alcaly. Poor now has a wide open court into which to hit his shot.

on the backhand, even if your shot will be played in the forehand side of the court. The further across you come with your opponent boxed up behind you, the wider open the court becomes.

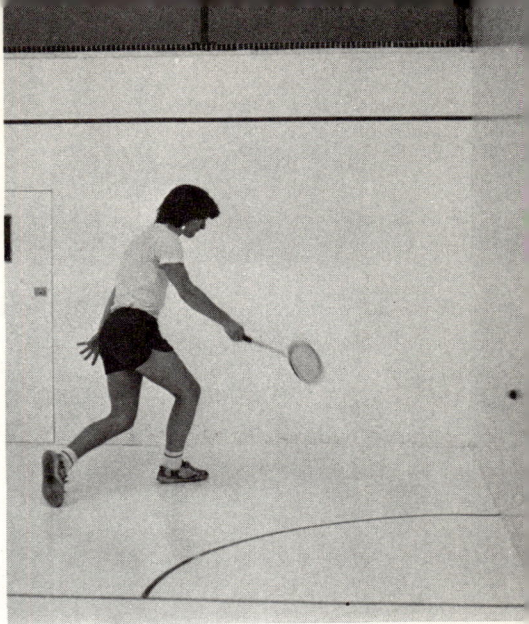

The racquet begins to swing across in front of the body as the ball hits the sidewall.

Practice using the boast to preserve your position on the "T." You can use it to return alley shots or crosscourt passes that get past you. This is a difficult concept for many people to grasp. If a ball gets past them, it immediately seems necessary to chase it back, to try somehow to get between it and the back wall once again. Many people try so hard that they hurt themselves in collisions and still can't get the ball back. Remember you don't have to hit the ball *directly* onto the front wall, so there is no reason to be between the ball and the back wall all the time.

Stand on the "T" and hit a ball down the forehand side of the court. Wait till the ball has got past you, then step back toward it with the left leg, (though when you're playing the shot for real, you'll often use the right instead). Swing the racquet across your leg and hook the ball onto the sidewall and thence onto the front. Keep your waist and your hips loose and let your head follow the ball on its way to the front left hand corner. As it does, your weight will return to the right leg, your left foot will be extricated, and you'll be standing high and dry back on the "T."

Don't tamper with the footwork on the backhand. Use your right leg to go back with. Visualize the photograph of Heather McKay on page 89. The difficulty with this variation of the shot is getting used to the idea of stepping back instead of forwards or sideways. It will require plenty of concentration to start with.

Gretchen Spruance goes back from the "T" on her left leg to recover a drive from Sue Newman of Australia.

Clive Caldwell, on the other hand, goes back on his right leg. Aziz Khan watches him closely.

Feed some balls further back, so you have to take a couple of strides to reach them. When you can get them back from there in a match, it'll have to be a good shot to get past you. This type of cut-off boast can be made in the air, but wait a while before trying that.

You're now ready for the big one, and if you were doing the cut-off boast correctly, it shouldn't be too much of a transition.

The balls you'll be dealing with are in the back corners. They would defeat your efforts to volley, and are impossible to return on the bounce directly to the front wall owing to apparent lack of room to swing the racquet. They will usually be serves or cross-court lobs which have come across, hit the sidewall near the back, and bounced too close to the back wall to be hit straight up the court. *But* they *can* go back the same way.

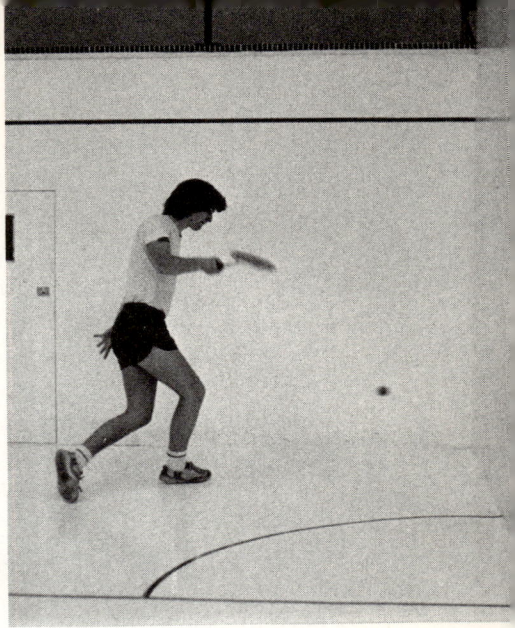

As the ball comes across toward the front forehand corner, the body begins to swing round with the racquet.

The first thing is to make yourself room. Nine times out of ten this means backpeddling. If you just stand there, the ball will squirt out of the sidewall and across you (or into your knees) before you can move the racquet. Don't get drawn across to the corner as the ball moves toward it. You can't swing a racquet in a corner anyway. Don't stand sideways. If the ball is tight with the back wall and you're sideways on, you'll hit the back wall with your racquet. Just line up parallel with the flight of the ball as you

The correct stance for the boast out of the back corner. Notice that from the position illustrated on the left, the player is not allowing room for a complete swing. From the correct position (illustrated on the right), the player has turned his body and has room for a complete swing.

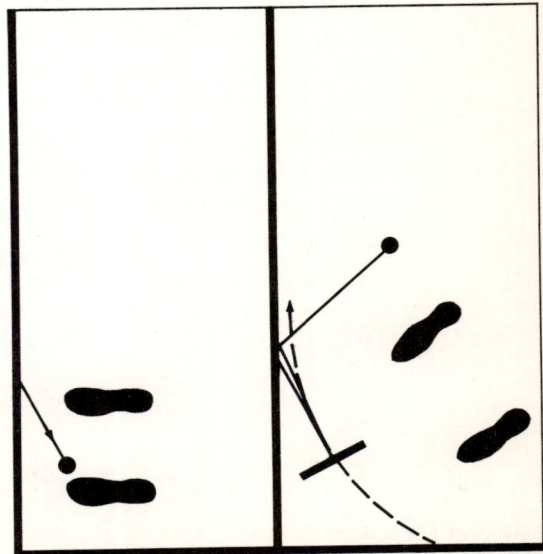

would with any other stroke. As it hits the sidewall, it changes direction. You must change the configuration of your body so that you are still standing parallel with the line of the ball after its deflection, and can swing down that line. Having turned your body to match the new direction of the ball, you can now hit it back the way it came. As you hit the ball, swing around to follow your shot to the opposite front corner; it will assist the hooking motion of the stroke.

Along the way the problem of crashing the racquet into the walls is largely alleviated. You can go much further and more effectively into a corner by swinging into it from outside than by standing in it. If you turn your body and move back as the ball comes off the sidewall, you'll be able to pick your racquet up and swing it in peace.

There are two ways to learn this particular shot. The first is with a partner. If you can get someone to feed you crosscourt lobs, you'll soon work this one out. On your own, you can bounce a few balls in the corners and get used to the motion; take half a dozen balls and it will speed things up. (See also "Drills.")

Remember, you don't necessarily have to hit the ball hard to recover it. With the boast from a corner, there is an advantage in not doing so. The shot is likely to wind up close to the edge of the court if you don't slam it and the interval between the swing of your racquet and the ball plopping onto the front wall can be disconcerting to your opponent.

Most players, when they learn to boast, are boast-happy for a couple of weeks, as the shot is so much fun to play. Playing too many makes you predictable, and a shot that ends in the front of the court really shouldn't be that. However, boasting, if used correctly, is one of the classic ways of destroying your opponent's rhythm and emphasizing your own, probably the safest way of bringing someone to the front, and the only effective way of escaping from the back corners.

Playing the boast is one of the marks of sophistication in a squash player. You may feel, having learned it, that you've mastered the game.

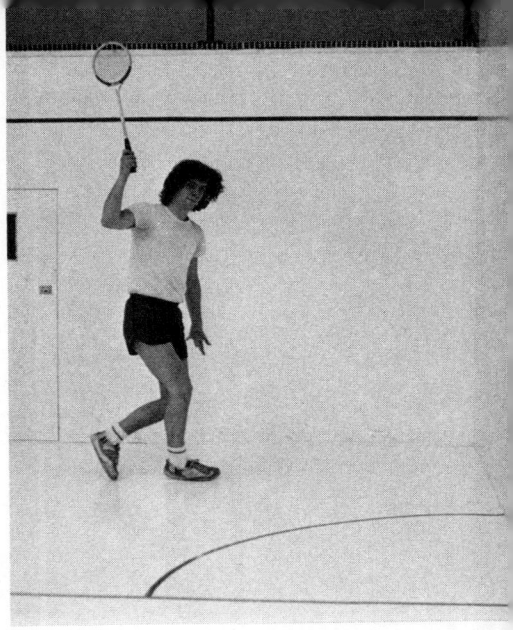

At the end of the stroke the body has come all the way round and has hooked itself out of the corner along with the ball.

9

THE LOB, THE DROP SHOT, REVERSE ANGLES

These are the three remaining strokes. Two of them, the lob and the drop shot, should be incorporated into any player's game; the third is only occasionally of value.

The lob and the drop shot have always been essential in the English game, but since the emergence of 70-plus, they have assumed greater importance in the American. If you're going to be an artist, you'll show it most clearly through these two shots. The bread and butter stuff is over. Here's the jam. If you're having a good day, you can tear anyone up with lobs and drops without appearing to try. Many young players consider them to be old man's tactics, a denial of the physical character of squash; they go on court, inwardly scoffing, and emerge in half an hour with egg on their faces.

The lob and the drop shot are touch shots. They must both be played, therefore, with the maximum of "feel" in the stroke. The danger with both is that they can become too mechanical. The player clenches as he sees a likely ball, jerks at it, and gives the

Gil Mateer aims a drop shot to the front forehand corner with Jay Nelson trapped behind him.

Even before the ball arrives for a lob, the racquet should be tilted upwards. (Photo by Benjamin Reeve.)

point away. The key to both shots is to be relaxed. Many players involved in a hard, fast game forget these shots exist. In an openly aggressive frame of mind it is often difficult to play delicately. But remember, nothing is more infuriating or exhausting than chasing to the front for a drop and then to the back for a lob. These are the thinking person's slots. When they win they quite clinically destroy their opponents, and there is a great deal of satisfaction in that.

Both strokes, as we have said, require the player to be relaxed during execution. Also, as part of their merit should be their disguise, the forehand and backhand lob and drop should be indistinguishable in their preparation from any other shot on the forehand or backhand wings.

For the lob, the racquet, gripped loosely, is released from the high ready position, and swings gently down catching the ball on the way up, well in front of the front leg. The ball will then sail up over your opponent's head, hit the sidewall in the case of a crosscourt, and bounce inside the back wall, giving your opponent little room to recover it.

The drop shot is a more difficult shot to perfect, since greater accuracy is required. Again the racquet is released from the high position, swings slowly down (the speed of this shot is obviously crucial), and cuts into the ball at about the same point as would a normal forehand or backhand. The cut is designed to bring the ball down as quickly as possible when it hits the front wall. (See diagram in "Advanced Techniques.")

Both shots require, as usual, a considerable amount of practice. *Don't* use them until you're confident of success. If they're off, they'll cost you the game.

These two shots, as you may have gathered, are logical partners. Used in conjunction they can exploit the court's greatest dimension, its length, to disrupt your opponent's rhythm.

Here is a typical scenario. In the fourth game of a match that has already lasted 45 minutes, "the screamer" feels that perhaps with one more rush of blood he will flap you for the last time. He plays the strokes you've seen a million times a little harder, and rushes forward in the court a little faster. You notice his clothes are saturated, his mouth is hanging open, and his face is puce. You smile to yourself. He plays out of a corner to the front and dashes forward to the "T." You obscure his vision of the ball as you move for it. He edges forward, suspiciously. You throw a lob crosscourt onto his backhand. He rushes back, recovers, and you hear him snorting behind you again. Twice more you throw up the lob, he reaches for those agonizing high backhands and you can see the fear on his face. The fourth time he's punchy. Once again, waiting till the last possible second, you drop the ball in the front forecourt corner and win the point.

Straight drop shots are the safest—they will stay close to the wall even if hit too high or too fast. If the ball comes out of the forehand corner, play it back there. The same for the backhand. Crosscourt drops are often marvelous for wrong-footing opponents, but if you're inaccurate, they just stand up in the middle to be hit. Don't play *any* drops from deep in the court. Unless you take your

Cutting through the ball on a backhand drop shot. (Photo by Benjamin Reeve).

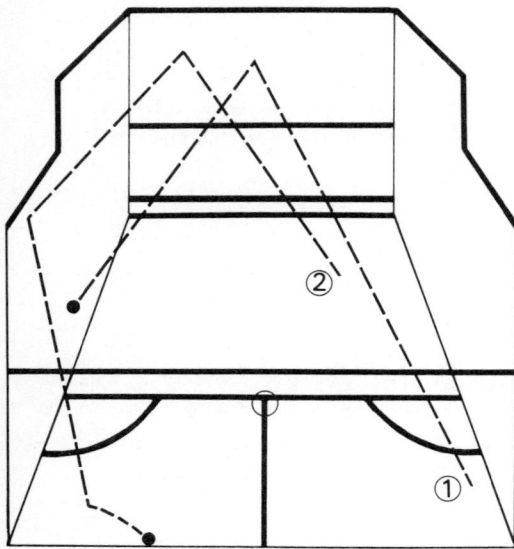

(1) is the wrong position for a lob. The ball can easily pass too close to the "T" and then be dropped short by the opponent. (2) is a good position. From here it is easy to put the ball over the head of the opponent at the "T" and force him to the back.

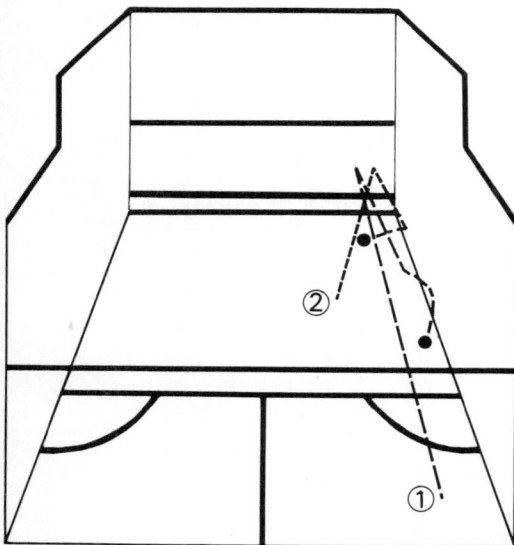

A drop shot from position (1) is more likely to be inaccurate; if it is, a player at the "T" has plenty of time and a lot of room to win the point. A drop shot from position (2) is good because it drags the opponent from the "T" even when it's inaccurate. Because you are closer to the target, you've a much better chance of being accurate.

opponent completely by surprise or hit a nick, he or she will be there before you're back in position. It is dangerous too, to play a crosscourt lob from deep in the court. The ball can easily pass within reach of the player at the "T." As soon as you master these two strokes and work them into your game, you'll start to get devious.

Reverse angle shots should aim to befuddle your opponent by their speed and sudden change of direction. They are used in the front of the court, on either forehand or backhand, and are supposed to look like crosscourts to your opponent standing behind. Instead of hitting a crosscourt, hit the ball earlier across your body, into the *opposite* sidewall so it will rebound off the front wall in front of you.

The reverse angle is easy to play; the footwork for it can be unashamedly lazy, and it is usually played from an open stance. It follows that the easier a shot, the less valuable it is, and that is the case here. The risks are that you might not deceive your opponent or that the ball will end up within reach of the center of the court. The one advantage, particularly with the 70-plus ball, is that you might hit a nick as the ball comes back across. In an even match between two good players, this shot might be used twice.

It is interesting to compare the reverse angle with the attacking boast, which can usually be played from the same position. From behind, the player shaping for a boast could also be playing an alley shot (among others). For a reverse angle, the only other possibility is a crosscourt.

Gil Mateer takes great care with his drop shot; Tom Page begins the race to cover it.

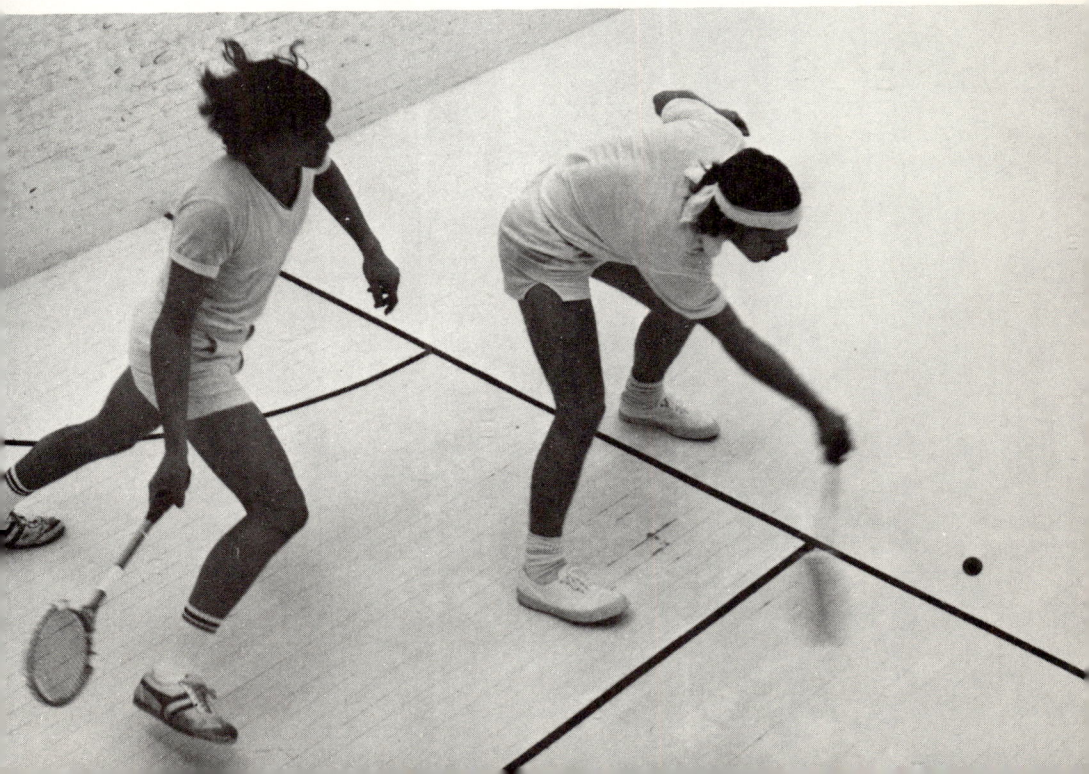

So, as shown below, player A's opponent, standing on the "T," can see two possible shots for A, as can B's opponent for B.

You will notice that the two possibilities for player B are a good deal closer than for player A. If an opponent is standing between the end points of B's two possible strokes, he can retrieve either. Not so with A's shots, where an opponent has to guess right.

All three of the shots in this chapter can be played in the air, but are a good deal more difficult that way.

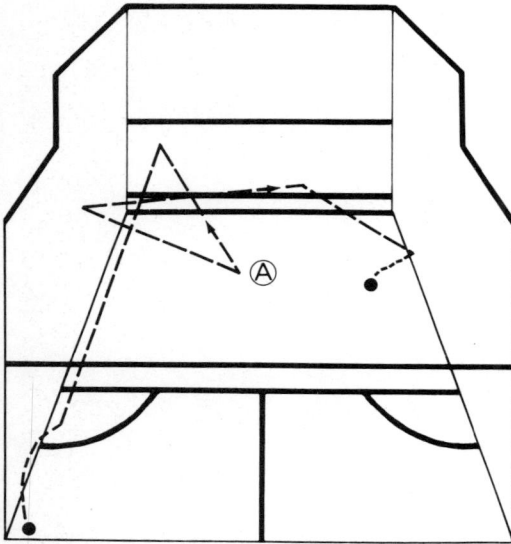

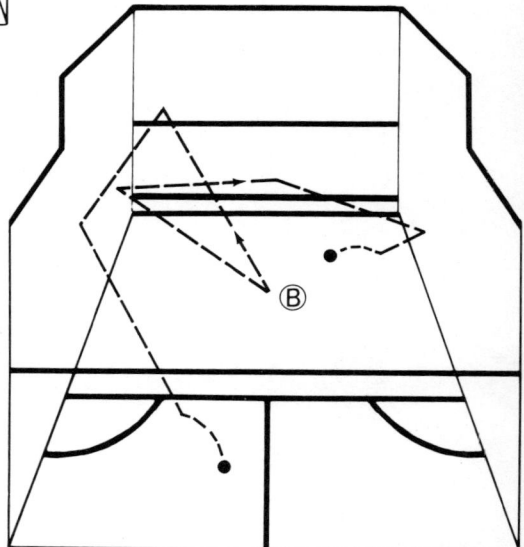

Victor Niederhoffer using his delicate touch on the way to beating Gul Khan in the Boodles British Gin Open (1976).

10

ADVANCED TECHNIQUES

We have dealt with the basic mechanics of the game; this chapter deals with a handful of ideas whose absence could prevent you from performing effectively on court.

COURT COVERING

There are certain areas on the court where you should never stand. These areas are no good for two reasons: it is impossible to use your racquet effectively standing inside them; you'll be too far out of position to have a reasonable chance of recovering.

If you move across to the edge of the court to play a shot, you need room to swing the racquet and an area into which to hit the ball. If you go too far across, your shot will fly into the middle, as you no longer have any space between you and the wall to play an alley shot into. In addition, going too far, either on the forehand or the backhand, almost always means taking a check pace on the *wrong* foot, *after* the correct one has been placed. You will find yourself throwing your weight across behind the ball as you hit it,

Stu Goldstein races around Mohibullah Khan on his way to the front of the court.

maybe colliding with the wall, and hooking everything across to where your opponent is standing.

Measure your strides; land with the *correct* foot on the edge of the bad side wall zones, and *stretch*—don't take another step. If you stick to this rule, the court will instantly seem smaller.

The same applies to the back wall region, except you can't be so dogmatic about the correct footwork. Many players who have watched other players boast the ball out of the corners and can see how it's done struggle blindly when they try. You need *room* for the racquet to swing. So, when going back, stop before you get there. You're aiming to reach into the corner with the racquet, not to stand there yourself; to have an easy passage back to the "T" when you've recovered the ball.

MOVING FROM THE "T"

Don't move from the "T" unless you have to. To stay there you must hit accurately and to a good length down the sidewalls. Avoid shots that pass through the middle region of the court. However, to win a point or move your opponent around, you sometimes have to attempt other things that involve venturing from the "T," and the response to them by your opponent might drive you well away. But even at a distance, all your movements should be made with the "T" in mind.

Every move you make on court should be made as a radius of the center of the "T." For example, if you go across to make a backhand, your last stride will be onto your right leg, which will stretch out toward the ball. Then you play your shot, and the right leg retracts directly towards the center of the "T," bringing your weight with it. Having played your shot from the edge of the court, you're in perfect position once again to play whatever comes next. The same should happen when you move forward or back. The last step toward the ball is the crucial one and will determine your direction when you start to come back. Movement on court is not just a matter of chasing balls like a maniac up and down and side to side.

Another key to apparently effortless court covering has nothing to do with fleetness of foot. Perhaps you stand on the "T" and stare straight ahead during points. When you see the ball, you career after it and come to grief. The reason for this is that you stare at

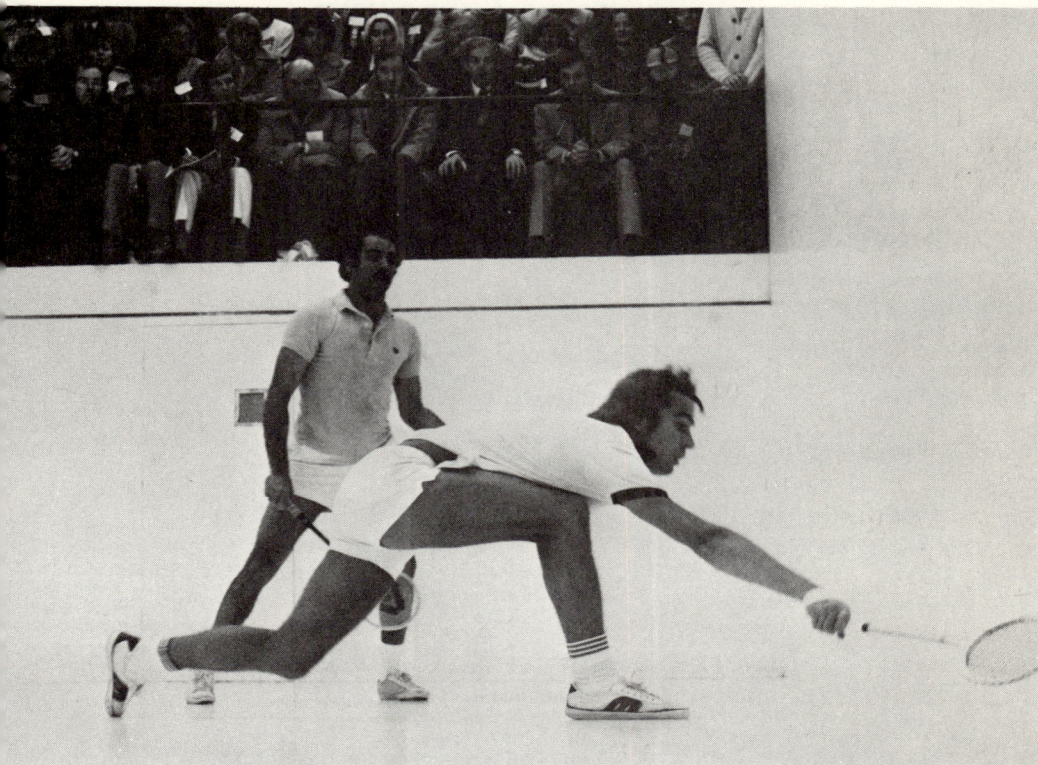

World Champion Geoff Hunt stretches right across from the "T" to the backhand wall for Sharif's alley shot. (1977 North American Open; Sharif went on to win.)

the front wall while the ball is behind you, then try to react after it strikes the front wall without enough time to be poised for a good shot.

Anyone in front of an opponent should turn and watch him shape up for his shot. If you do, you'll have a much better and earlier indication of where to go for *your* next shot. As effective deception is unlikely from the back half of the court, you can very often arrive where you opponent has aimed the ball before it even gets there. This form of elementary anticipation can rapidly demoralize a less experienced player, and make your game much easier.

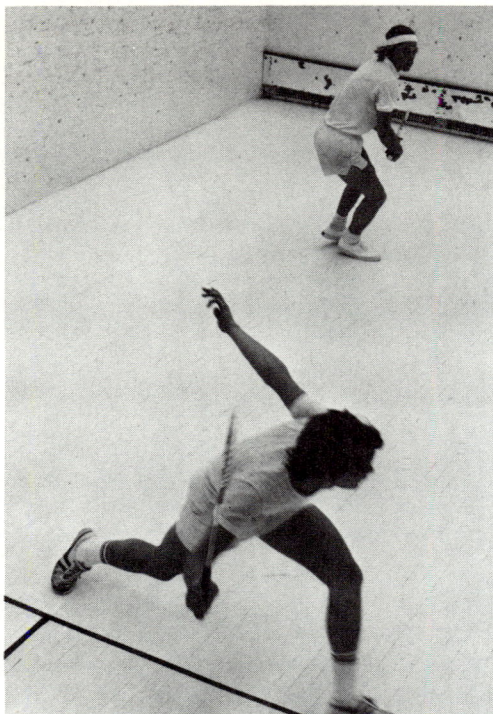

Tom Page at the "T" stretches across to play
a forehand winner against Gil Mateer.

Mike Desaulniers, an upcoming champion, manages to retain his position at the "T" despite
Joe Swain's accurate alley shot.

DECEPTION

Everyone will have their favorites among the shots discussed in the technique section, and a predisposition to play them whenever possible. "My God, you should see my backhand crosscourt this week—wait till I get you on the court with it." It's important to realize that no matter in what position you find yourself, you'll usually have a choice of what shot to play. Your opponent almost always has to guess. When you're under pressure, his or her guess is probably going to be accurate, as the alternatives to the easiest shot are difficult. But if you have an easy ball bouncing towards the "T," or an easy volley, you have *seven* alternatives. Remember, however, it is one of the costliest mistakes not to vary your shots and *use* all seven. If you don't, you make your opponent's job of anticipation a great deal easier.

Don't panic—it's even worse to go onto the court with seven shots in mind, get up front, and hit the ball limply into your own legs.

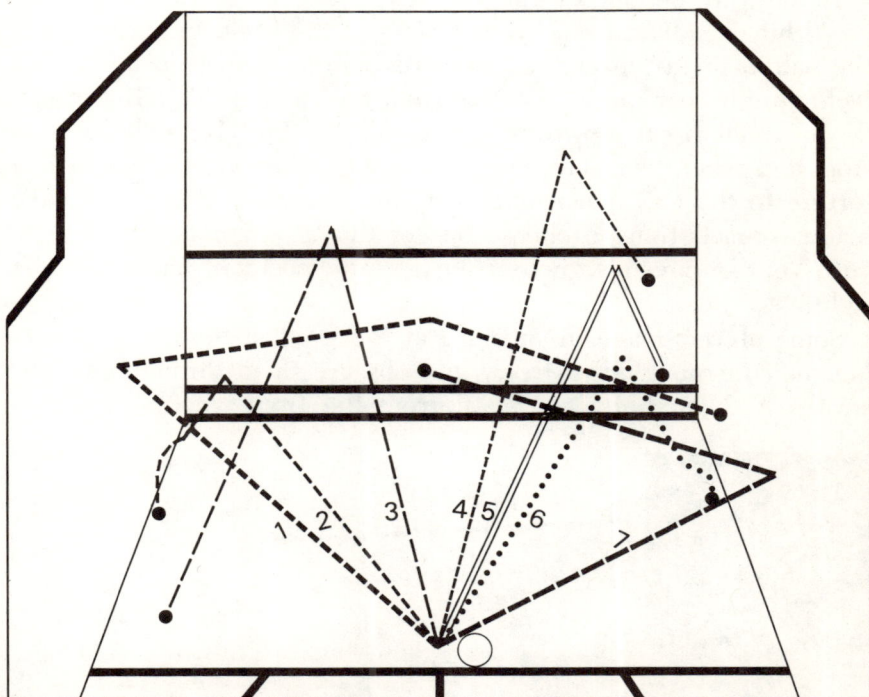

The seven alternatives: (1) boast; (2) straight drop shot; (3) alley shot; (4) cross-court lob; (5) crosscourt; (6) crosscourt drop; (7) reverse angle.

One condition that leads to a lack of inventiveness in winning positions is the overkill instinct. "Hey, here we go, here's an easy one—this one's going right through the wall—Reg won't know what hit him." The ball can only be hit in one direction when the player rushes in and hammers the thing with all his might. Reg will be ready for the ball long before it arrives unless he or she is intimidated by your heavings. Pure speed does not win points very often. In a squash court the ball has far too many opportunities to slow down.

Two techniques will help you deceive your opponent. The first is masking the ball, and the second is leaving the stroke until the last possible moment. The first is more natural than the second and should be used when possible everywhere on court.

If you can mask the ball, your opponent will be less sure of his movements, and consequently a little slower to the ball, than otherwise. Masking, as you can see in the pictures (see below), amounts simply to putting your body between the ball and your opponent to obstruct vision of your shot. You're then in a position to do something subtle like turning the racquet head.

If you wait too long for the ball, trying to deceive your opponent, you'll hit it badly. Stretch your timing to the limit, but try to take the ball at or just after the top of its bounce. (Keep in mind, this technique is very rarely effective from behind the "T.") If you can do it, you'll break up your opponent's rhythm. He will have to stop, and when you finally play your shot, start again (which is a torture to the legs, particularly late in a match). Also, you'll have made yourself time to choose one of the seven shots available to you. Your opponent's guess, from a static position, had better be right.

Some players make the mistake at the front of the court, of taking their racquets down to try and obscure them throughout their stroke. A drop shot, or a boast from the front, should resemble

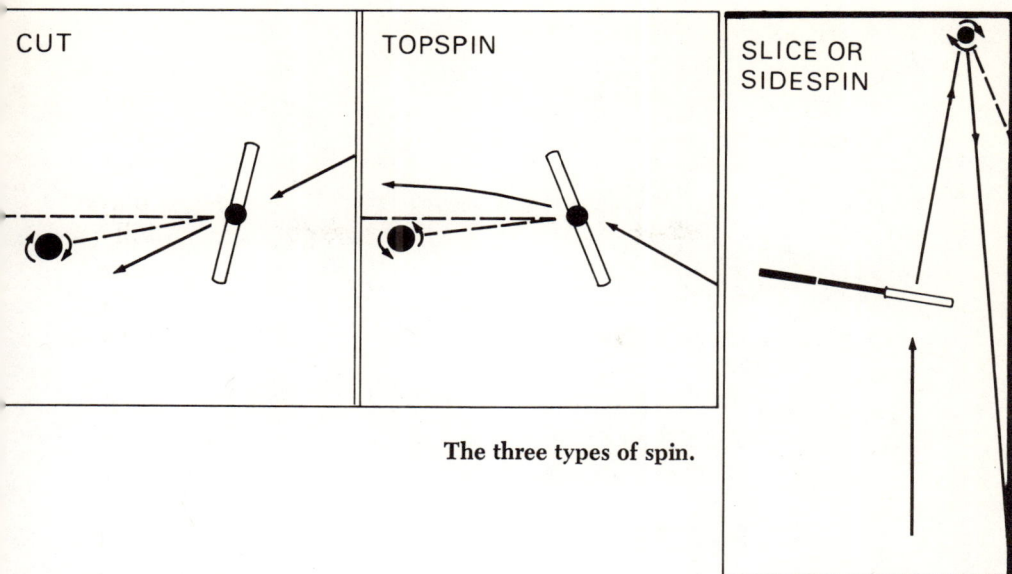

| CUT | TOPSPIN | SLICE OR SIDESPIN |

The three types of spin.

other strokes. A drive to the back, to be consistently accurate, should have a nice, high backswing, and should be hit as fiercely and as suddenly as possible. Thus, dropping the racquet to be extra-sneaky is not a good idea.

Finally, don't be too cute too often—don't play too many drops and angles. Most of the court is behind you, and while you might get satisfaction out of the moves, when they're repetitive they're easy to predict, and leave the ball conveniently in the front of the court for your opponent to dispose of.

SPIN

Spin does not play so great a part in squash as in other games. After a ball has hit a wall and reaced a player, any spin the striker puts on it is neutralized. However, it does have two important applications. First, "cut" (one type of spin) can bring the ball down for a drop shot or short kill. Second, "slice" (another type of spin) can straighten the ball with the sidewall on an alley shot. (See diagram above.) This technique becomes instinctive after enough play, so don't worry about it.

Occasionally, with the English ball, crosscourt drop shots are played with top spin to carry them further across toward the nick, but such sophistry is rare, and unnecessary.

11

PLAYING TO WIN

The ability to win consistently is the acid test of your involvement with the game. Very few players enjoy losing all the time—squash is the next best thing to prizefighting for competing egos. No revenge is sweeter than reversing a previous defeat, no triumph more glorious than beating someone who was ahead, for justice is at last being served.

If you win, squash suddenly becomes the graceful, exciting game you knew it was. The beauty that formerly escaped you is in the fact that squash has no excuses—it is raw combat moderated by neutral rules. You defeat your opponent on a basic level which the mechanics of the game cannot disguise. If you lose, you have no one to blame but yourself.

Either role can become habitual, but after a time most people manage to break out of them. It's too much strain winning all the time, and losing, despite its attractiveness to some, can finally be a little demoralizing. The intriguing thing about losing is that even after a deal of self-examination, in a close match it is impossible to come up with a good reason for it. Why were you turning all your backhand drops into setups? Why, when you knew how to

Sharif Khan is the winner and Victor Niederhoffer the runner-up in the 1976 North American Open.

World champion Geoff Hunt with an imperious forehand.

beat the nasty, compulsive little swine, didn't you? Going to more general excuses, why weren't you as fit, why didn't you practice?

There is a simple answer: you wanted to lose. It wasn't that at the crucial time, you didn't want to win *as much* as your opponent; you didn't want to win *at all*. The root cause for losing to someone you could beat, and, by extension, everyone else, is a failure of confidence. Realizing you can beat someone is easier for some people than actually doing it. Certain players get over this by proclaiming their superiority and thereby assuming the responsibility to demonstrate it. But self-promotion is as bad as making excuses. It betokens the same lack of confidence. Having said you'll beat someone, you step out on a limb. You've attracted everyone's attention, which might suit you, but they're all gaping at you, waiting for a fall. And your opponent enjoys nothing more than cutting down arrogant upstarts. The pressure that is created is artificial. If you didn't believe you could win without bragging (and obviously you didn't), you stand to do much worse by your confidence than by losing with your mouth shut.

Don't open your mouth before, during, or after your match, unless, as it is in progress, you feel like complimenting one or two of your opponent's shots. Don't argue with the referee. Don't claim lets all the time. (See rules.) Don't get mad if your opponent cheats, just quietly suggest that he's wrong, and if he persists, don't play him again. Every time you open your mouth, you give yourself away, and your style of playing reveals quite enough of your personality. In a match, it is vital to be isolated from your opponent. If you realize that winning and losing are both entirely your responsibility, such discipline shouldn't be hard.

If the reason for losing is a failure of confidence, you have to improve it before you can win. If it's just one match against one person that you lose, you might snap back when next you play. But, if you persist in losing to one person, or have a run of losses to a series of different people, something needs to be done.

Losing is lazy—laziness is a lack of self-respect. Only by working can you pull yourself out of a losing run. If you remove all your excuses for losing (not fit, injured, out of practice, didn't know he did that so well), you might start winning again.

FITNESS

To know that you can run hard throughout a match is reassuring. But you have to take the game seriously enough to invest the effort. Until you do, losing will be easy. Initially you may play squash to get fit. After a certain point it will make as much sense to get fit to play squash. That point marks the beginning of a serious desire to win.

Different training routines have different virtues. For the strength required in the ankles and the knees and for repeated short-distance acceleration, there are a couple of exercises:

1) Short-distance interval training. Sprint 30–50 yards (mark the distance first), pause for ten seconds, then sprint back. Continue this for as long as you can. Count your sprints, then go back next time and do more.
2) On court. Stand on the "T" with the racquet. During a

timed period, which you should steadily increase, sprint from the "T" to the corner, play an imaginary shot, return to the "T," then move immediately to another corner. Keep this up, each time passing from one corner through the "T" to the next. Occasionally play a mock cut-off. Face the front each time you pass through the "T" until the time elapses. A minute is a suitable amount to begin with. This is an exceedingly grueling exercise that bears fruit in direct proportion. It's even better if someone helps you. Number the corners, and have the other person call the numbers at random, urging speed from you. Count the corners as you go. The next time you play, if you've recovered, you'll reach a lot of balls without knowing how you did it.

For strength in the back, try repeated overhead lifting from the floor of *light* weights (up to 20 lbs.) without bending your knees.

For strength in the racquet arm, repeat 5–10 lb. dumbbell lifts from the elbow or shoulder.

Other less specialized exercises are sit-ups, leg-raises, push-ups,

See "2" above.

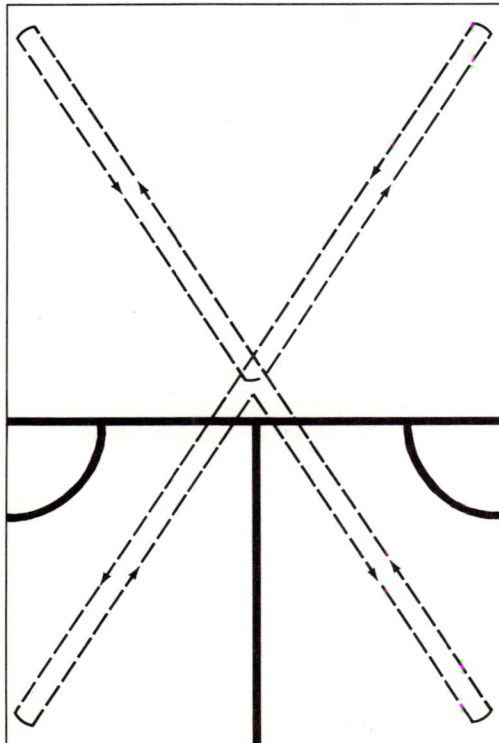

and step-ups (onto a bench and down and up). They are helpful, but do not yield quick results. They are more useful for the essential off-court warm-up which drastically reduces the risk of muscle, tendon, and ligament injuries.

Many of the best players skip rope to good effect for nimbleness on court.

Running long distances is helpful for stamina and heart and lung strength. Don't expect to run one week and see your game improve the next. If anything, after such a short time, you'll be worse off—your legs will have lost their snap, you'll be slower off the mark and slower round the court. Only after a period of months does distance work pay off, but it can give you the basic endurance, if not the power, to succeed.

PRACTICE

You must play a particular shot accurately enough and often enough in practice to be completely confident that you can play it under pressure. If you tend to screw up a certain shot, practice it until it's coming out of your ears, until the idea of making easy errors on it is quite fantastic *to you*.

DIET

You need a balanced diet with plenty of protein and carbohydrates for muscle and for the energy to be used in that muscle—but most people eat more than they need anyway. The only things to avoid are a lot of alcohol or cigarettes, especially during the forty-eight hours before a match.

The only diet that has been shown significantly to augment the amount of energy available to the player is one in which, during the week-and-a-half before a match, until the last two days, you eat no carbohydrates *at all*, sticking solely to vegetables and protein. The body builds up a big carbohydrate gap which, during the last two days or so, you fill as fast as you can, stuffing yourself with sweet junk foods of all descriptions. If the timing is right, you get a carbohydrate high, for what it's worth.

Don't eat immediately before a game. Digestion ceases almost completely with the so-called "vascular shunt" to the outer muscles, and the lump in your guts is uncomfortable when you're running. Don't drink too much in between games for the same reason—you don't want a lot of water sloshing about.

PREPARING FOR A MATCH

You're fit, well-practiced, temperate, and now you have to think about a specific match.

First, the location. How long will it take to get there? Plan to arrive in time to change and warm-up, not so early as to be hanging about, not so late as to keep your opponent waiting. Are the courts warm or cold; i.e. is it likely to be a running game, or full of winners and short rallies?

Next, your opponent. You don't want to know who he (or she) has beaten, just who he's lost to and why. You want to know what he does badly and what well to establish a mental pattern of his game. Is he a hitter, a retriever, a front-court player? Unless you're irrepressibly curious, you shouldn't watch your opponent play. It's a mistake to make too much of a study of him. The opposition always looks better from the gallery.

Having stretched and warmed up, go on court with the idea that your opponent doesn't exist. He's simply there to offer you the ball to hit so it won't come back. It's as simple as that. You'll win 3–0 in twenty minutes. Use the warm-up to make sure you're loose, and remember you can't win the match yet. Then get going, feel the adrenalin, think incisively, enjoy it, and don't let up.

If things go wrong, *stay cool*. Don't let your opponent see you're perplexed or tired—any sign from you that he's doing well will help him. Pull yourself *out* of the physical anguish and the uncomfortable pattern that has developed. Change your game; do something sudden—a hard serve, a hard low boast, a very slow drop shot, lobs —anything to change the character of the match. If you're winning, don't change a thing. If it's tight near the end, one of the best ways of encouraging yourself is to look at your opponent: see how he's suffering and your own discomfort will be alleviated. Take *more* trouble rather than less as a close match goes on. The later you push yourself in such a match, the better your chance of breaking your weakened opponent. It's remarkable how many people will give up in the fifth game. It's easy to resign when you're in the fifth and tired, feeling you're done enough to acquit yourself. After all, you *did* "try." Close only counts in horseshoes.

In the end, you're bound to lose sometimes, but you wouldn't play very often and wouldn't enjoy it much if you expected to. Any real commitment to the game implies a desire to win. When you're struggling to win, you're struggling to enjoy yourself. If you can succeed on a squash court, it can make life seem very simple.

12

WOMEN'S SQUASH

Ten years ago, when squash had its place with hot towels and massages in gentlemen's clubs, there were scarcely any women playing squash in America. Since that time, with the opening of commercial metropolitan clubs, the situation has been transformed.

To the enormous number of working women and housewives, the release of a quick squash game at lunchtime or after work has proved convenient and useful. In short, there is *no* reason why women's squash, which can have all the grace and poise of women's tennis, should not have the same importance relative to the men's game. As more and more women get serious about the sport, as the USWSRA continues to organize and the tournament circuit grows, such a situation is becoming increasingly inevitable. However, one does well to remember that it has not yet arrived, and that some men will always patronize.

If you're beginning the game, realize that the average woman is as coordinated and physically fit as the average man, and *relax*. If you begin to play at the same time as a man, don't wait for him to laugh at your mistakes and then hang up your bobble socks—laugh at his.

Marion Clement is ready to take this ball off the back wall.

At a high level, the physical differences between men and women begin to tell—men can hit the ball harder and run faster; but a few things show up the other way. Women are usually much quicker to spot and capitalize on a winning position and they play many more of the touch strokes that fascinate spectators.

Probably the best woman athlete in the world is a squash player —Heather McKay of Australia. She comes close to the very best male pros and hasn't lost a match to a woman in fifteen years. There are many ingredients of play at that level that can be incorporated into your game.

When playing men, don't try and play a man's game, don't try to out-hit him. The key to any squash victory is the calculated disruption of your opponent's pattern of play and the assertion of your own. Play your shot, not his. Concentrate on dragging him to the front and then pushing him back. Make him stretch. Hit the ball where he isn't. Try not to give away free speed on your shots, make him hit the ball. Above all, don't spare his pride.

Playing against men is a good way of developing the match-winning characteristics of your game. Speed and strength will be improved as a matter of course. The disruptive skills (drop shots, lobs, boasts, high serves) will benefit from the challenge.

Here are two technical points that might assist you. You might tend to stand upright when you play. If you try to move quickly and turn in an upright position, you won't be able to: your center of gravity will be far too high and your balance ruined. Even without moving for the ball, unless you bend your knee during a shot, you lose all the potential power of weight transference to the leading leg, and with it any poise and accuracy for your shot.

The versatile Diana Nyad forces Debbie Brickley to stretch.

The great Heather McKay.

Second, don't use a racquet that feels uncomfortably heavy which you might have bought either because it was cheap or because you thought you'd work through it. The most important time to have an appropriate racquet is when you're learning how to play. A heavy racquet has brought many men and women to the point of despairing of their prospects of ever overcoming beginner's awkwardness.

Mariann Greenberg uses a high grip.

Be conscious of the thickness of the handle. It should not be an effort to hold the racquet securely and swing it. Watch particularly for terry cloth grips. If you buy a racquet with one, make sure when you replace it that you remove the old toweling from the handle. *Don't* stick more on top.

To augment accuracy and control through your grip on the racquet simply move your hand toward the top of the handle until it feels right. What you sacrifice in power, you make up in precision and feel. *Don't* use two hands to support a racquet you can't control. Pick it right up on the backswing or get another.

Despite the massive ground swell of interest in squash among women, there are surprisingly few top women players. A bare handful the world over earn their livings playing tournament squash. Clearly this situation will change.

Already, women's squash has altered the character of the game. There's a color and excitement now that was lacking in the esoteric, baggy-shorted days.

13

SQUASH FOR THE TENNIS PLAYER

Increasing numbers of tennis players are moving to squash during the winter. When May comes round a lot of them don't want to stop, and for them squash becomes a year-round game. They are usually attracted by the sheer practical convenience of the game in comparison to tennis, particularly in cities. Half an hour during lunchtime or after work can get you as much exercise as an hour or so of singles tennis and God knows how much doubles. And you'll wind up spending much less money.

Squash is a game with at least as much subtlety as tennis, with fewer and shorter breakdowns in play, and with as much excitement. The social side of tennis has not yet been matched by squash, though large investors are falling over themselves to rectify that situation. The gap in popularity between the two games is because squash was only recently made widely accessible; and is still behind in media coverage; it has nothing to do with the respective merits of either game.

Sharif Khan at Rockefeller Center before the World Racquets Championship of 1977. Bjorn Borg was another contestant.

For whatever reason you come to play squash there are a lot of new things to learn. Many tennis players consider squash to be simply an idiosyncratic form of tennis played indoors. If you play tennis regularly, it will take time to acclimatize to the finer points of squash. But be patient—squash can provide enormous benefits in footwork, court covering, and coordination for your tennis game.

We'll start off with the grip. The lighter racquet, the rapid succession of shots, and the greater speed of the ball in squash mean that the grip cannot afford to be such a complicated matter as in tennis. I favor a grip which is a good deal more compact on the racquet handle than a tennis grip. It will enable you to deliver more speed more directly to the racquet head. Two more things. Once again for the sake of speed *forget* changing the grip from forehand to backhand. In squash your elbow and wrist are sufficiently loose to be able to compensate without that. In order to have your wrist and elbow loose, the first step is to grip the racquet much more loosely than you would for tennis. In that way you free the wrist and elbow during the stroke. You're generating speed from your arm's two levers, the wrist and the elbow, not from a lot of body turn and a stiff arm as you're used to.

The swing in squash is much more compact. Squash is played in a confined space beside another player, so precision is necessary. As I have said in the technique chapters, the only point where the arm and the racquet are in a straight line is at the point of impact —before and after that point they are unwinding to it or winding up beyond it. If you go onto a squash court with a tennis swing, which occupies twice the space, you'll soon hit your opponent or wreck your racquet. If you have problems with bending your arm, think of throwing a rock on the forehand and a frisbee on the backhand and read the applicable technique chapter.

In the squash grip, as opposed to the tennis grip, the hand is much more compact. But in both cases, the index finger provides control during the swing. (Photo by Benjamin Reeve.)

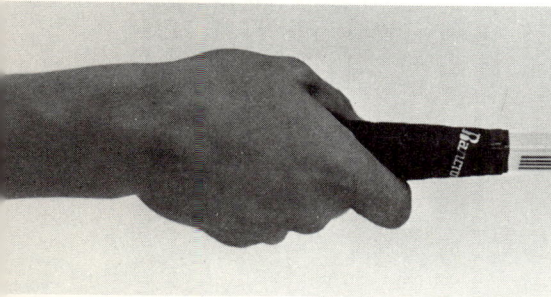

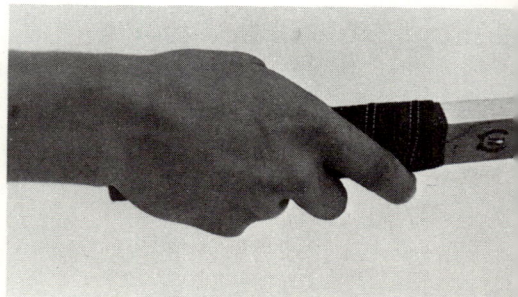

Stu Goldstein winding up for a backhand from deep in the court.

Another aspect of tennis instinct is detrimental to squash—that of holding the racquet in both hands before the stroke. Squash racquets are not heavy enough to require this, and the habit becomes serious, particularly on the backhand when pressure is built up against the supporting hand which is released at the desired point of impact like a catapult. The ball goes all over the place. *Just one hand.*

Now the serve. Although the hard serve in squash is hit as hard as a tennis serve, the spin is unnecessary. After hitting the front wall, any spin you've lavished on the ball will be neutralized and have no effect on your opponent. Unless you hit a nick, all shots in squash are bouncing predictably by the time they reach your op- up against the supporting hand which is released at the desired ponent. The uses of spin are described in "Advanced Techniques." Don't throw the ball up. You don't have to hit it down over a net.

Even the volleys in squash, which are made with a stroke that considerably resembles the tennis volley, are different in that a defensive volley in squash is hit upwards.

Movement on court is probably the trickiest, though most stimulating, difference between tennis and squash. Right away you'll discover you have to move more quickly over a shorter distance and lower to the ground and that pressure on your ankles and

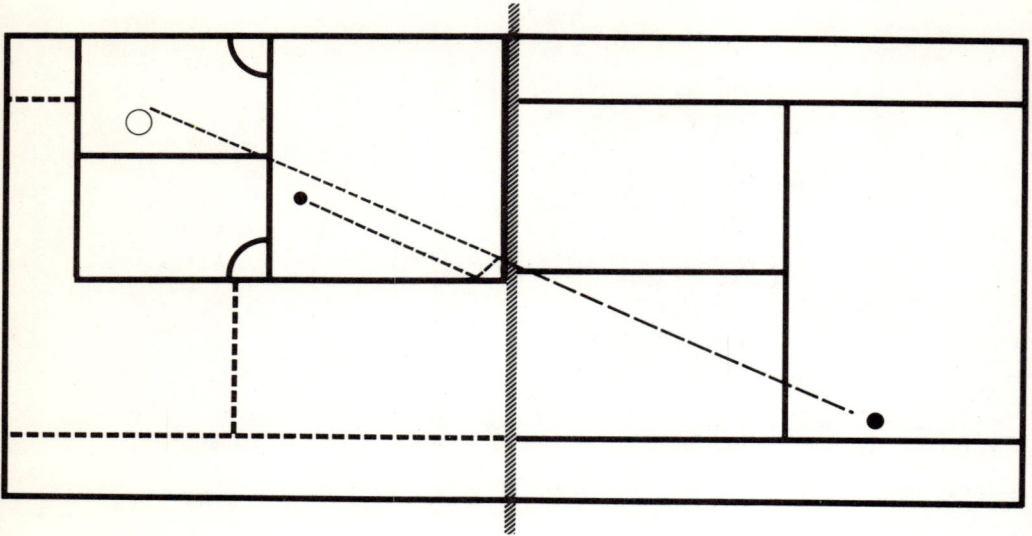

The tennis court vs. the squash court.

knees is much greater, especially as you should stop dead as you make each shot. As I have already said, the squash swing has to be made closer to the body than the tennis swing for reasons of space. Movements on the court have to be made with the same control in mind. You can't go galloping after a ball without risking injury on the walls. Very often chasing the ball isn't even necessary —one that's running away from you is not beyond hope in this game—it can come back towards you from the side or back walls, and you can even return a ball that's gone past you with a boast. Squash may be a fast game, but it does not require the feverishness that ignorance of the moves and the assistance the walls provide can give it. Squash is not, then, a game played purely back to front down a channel marked by the sidewalls.

It is much more of a side-on game than tennis. Tennis players' most common problem is connected with this. There is an extreme urgency displayed to return to the front-on tennis ready position, ready to pounce whether the ball comes forehand or backhand. This urgency obscures both the intention and the execution of the shot.

Most tennis players hit the ball consistently when it is far from the walls, but not when it isn't. I've had looks that say, "You cheat," when I hit a ball toward the edge of a court. The front-on posture, then, both anticipates and precipitates a game in which the ball stays in the middle. Start thinking *side*-on, completing your stroke before coming back. Only for an instant should you ever stand front-on. (See technique chapters on forehand & backhand and "Advanced Techniques.")

Tennis players often think of the "T" as the net in tennis. As said above, it is not.

Just keep in mind as you play your shot that you can't rush to the "T"; face the front and merely wait. Watch where your shot goes, watch how your opponent shapes to hit the ball, and the game will be a lot easier. (See also "Advanced Techniques.")

By the time you've been on court for a while and become acquainted with the principles mentioned in this chapter, you'll already be hooked on the game. It may not be like tennis, but you'll find it a fascinating alternative.

Jay Nelson waiting for the ball to go round the back corner and come back towards him. Khalid Mir watches.

137

14

THE 70-PLUS GAME

When it was introduced at the end of the summer of 1977, this new ball was an approach by the United States Squash Racquets Association to the International Squash Racquets Federation which governs squash outside the United States and Mexico. It is now much more likely that there will be commerce between players of the two camps, and already many English ball stars have been lured to America by big purses and improved prospects of success.

Despite the arguments of diehards in both camps, it seems that in many ways the 70-plus combines the best features of the old hardball and the English ball. Rallies are no longer so short, but there remains the possibility of consistently putting loose balls away which on a hot court with an English ball is at least problematic. Shot-making, then, is at a premium. There is not only a wider range of "kills" than before, but also a wider variety of ways to create the opportunity for such shots. The old hardball game has at once been modernized and made more accessible. The introduction of 70-plus and the take-off of squash in America cannot really be separated.

A game that was basically rather a primitive slugging match has

David Linden and Peter Briggs caught in the kind of tangle that was common in hardball squash.

Squash balls (left to right). The old American hardball, which weighs 31.2 to 42.6 grams and has a diameter of 43.2 to 44.4 millimeters. The 70-plus ball is made from the same rubber as the hardball and has the same dimensions as the English ball; it weighs 19.3 to 21.6 grams, 45% less than the hardball. The English ball, which weighs 23 to 24.6 grams, has a diameter of 39.5 to 41.5 millimeters.

become a game with a greater capacity for flair and invention. This is the responsibility of a slower, smaller, softer, bouncier squash ball that comes in two grades—the blue dot for summer or for courts that are above about 70 degrees, hence the name, and the white dot, which is the livelier one, used in most tournaments and on colder courts or in cooler weather. In effect, a slower ball means a larger court. The ball now regularly finds its way into places it didn't often see before.

If you either used to be a hardball player or are now beginning the game, there are several features of the new ball to look at. First the serve.

The lob serve in 70-plus squash has a greater role than it did in the old game. A high serve used to cannon out of the corner it was aimed for and give the receiver a slow bouncing ball to hit; now, however, a well-directed lob serve kisses the sidewall high up and drops like a stone into the corner, where it is very hard to retrieve, harder even than an English ball.

It is now possible to penetrate to the corners with lower, flatter serves. In the old game these were blasted in at full pace, vaguely aimed to hit a point low on the sidewall or the back wall. This ploy can still be effective, but now has an alternative. On a serve to the forehand, if the low serve is weighted to bounce *between* the sidewall and the back wall, it will slow up and restrict the receiver's room to deal with it, or even die away altogether. The ball takes longer to go from racquet to racquet, and the server has a better opportunity of covering the next shot. Similar effects are now possible from the serve to the backhand with a flat backhand service. Both forms of backhand serve, the lob and the lower, faster type, have found a place in the 70-plus game which just wasn't there before. (See "Serving Chapter.")

The lobs and drop shots are now viable ways of discomfiting your opponent. In the old game both were usually signs of fatigue rather than devilment. The lob would usually either fly harmlessly out of court, or bounce out into the middle from the back wall. Not only the lob serve but also the lob itself can now be put into the back corners to stay; it can be used as an attacking move, and forces a technically more difficult defensive return than any required by the hard ball.

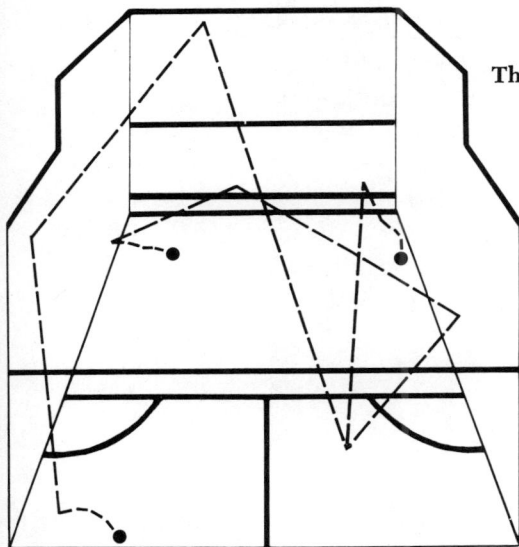

Three typical 70-plus bounces.

Three typical hardball bounces.

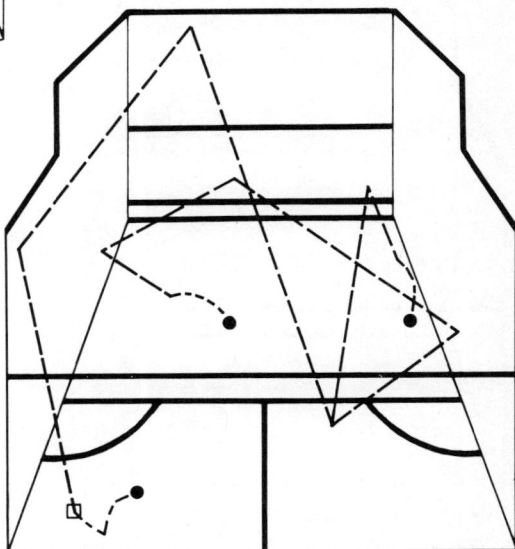

In 70-plus the straight drop shot has become one of the most obvious ways of winning a point. The old hardball drop nearly always turned it into a short alley to be punished by the opposition. But now, for the first time in America, the front of the court can be exploited. Rather than trying to drill a hole in your opponent's crosscourt covering, which was generally the case before, the whole length of the court is now available. The 70-plus drop shot can be cut to bring the ball down. The old hardball was simply too shiny and too heavy to grip effectively with the racquet.

Because of the same matte surface, and the new liveliness of the ball, the attacking boast assumes a new importance. After the ball has hit three walls, it's spinning like a top towards your opponent, and if it is hit low, it has a most satisfactory tendency to slide over towards the sidewall nick and scoot straight along the floor. The boast has become a shot with which it is possible to win a point from almost anywhere on court, although, as I said in the technique section, the odds against success become greater the further back you play it.

Hitting a three-wall boast (see diagram below) was a most unusual achievement with the hardball, but is a good deal more practical now. It will leave the ball as close to the front wall as it can possibly be, with almost no forward momentum. With it, you have another and even more effective way of exploiting the size of the court.

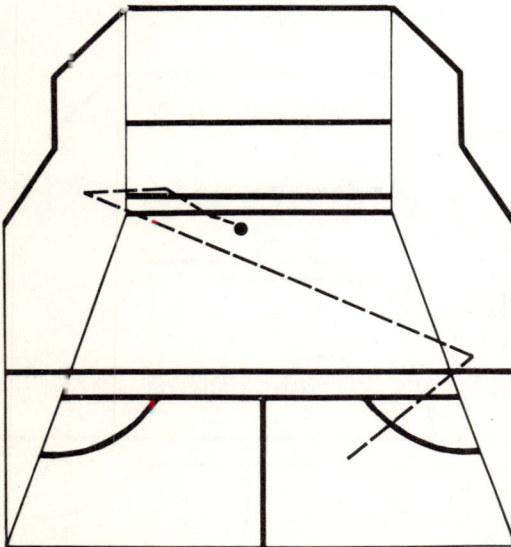

The three wall boast.

With the new possibilities of the lob serve, it is essential to be able to boast out of the corners. This can catch out ex-hardball players who scoop ridiculously instead of boasting. Because of the greater chance of playing the ball into the back corners and getting it to stay there, cutoff volleying from the "T" has become more important. It no longer makes as much sense to let the ball pass and hope it will return to you at the "T" from the back wall.

The 70-plus ball has made a considerable difference in the swing, at least for groundstrokes. Previously, with the faster, lower bouncing ball, most strokes were short-arm jabs. The backswing was abbreviated and the follow-through almost non-existent—there simply wasn't enough time to play anything but rather ugly strokes. With the extra time available now, the best players can at last exhibit crowd-pleasing qualities—a higher pick-up, a curved swing, a higher follow-through, and, for the most part, a more precisely struck ball. Players at club level can progress to low, hard drives and short kills much earlier and with more confidence than before, and can move on to new and subtler tactics which were outside the range of the old game.

Another improvement made by the 70-plus ball is that it makes the game more of a tactical challenge than a show of strength. Squash is no longer raw hacking and a cold shower; you have the time now to throw your opponent the wrong way and dispense with the rugged All-American stuff if it's distasteful to you.

The basic units of the hardball game—alley shots and crosscourts —retain their importance, but the 70-plus ball has brought with it some of the characteristics of that International game—the parabolic serve and lob, the straight drop shot, the corner boast, the attacking boast. There is more running, along with more strokes and more time to play them. The 70-plus ball may be a compromise, but it has a charm all its own.

15

THE ENGLISH GAME

The basic differences between the English and the American game would not, at first glance, appear to amount to much: the ball is softer and the court is a slightly different shape.

However, the character of the English game is completely different from American 70-plus, and is one which millions of devotees outside the United States believe is the purest. It antedates the American, and it is pretty difficult to explain the divergence in about 1890 on this side of the Atlantic, except to say that as the rules and structure of the game were not then properly formalized, and no particular code had the upper hand, it was considered that an American variation was as valid as any other, and might as well carry the day. As soon as both codes were formalized they closed ranks, and became intractable. At least until the introduction of 70-plus, the situation remained the same.

The English game has consolidated its hold on the rest of the world, and is considerably more advanced in its boom than the American game. For example, more people in Australia play squash regularly than play tennis. Now that the boom is beginning in America, clearly the interests of both federations, the International

Junior Mike McGuire of Montreal hits a forehand drive in an International ("English" ball) match against Jim Jefferies of Bermuda.

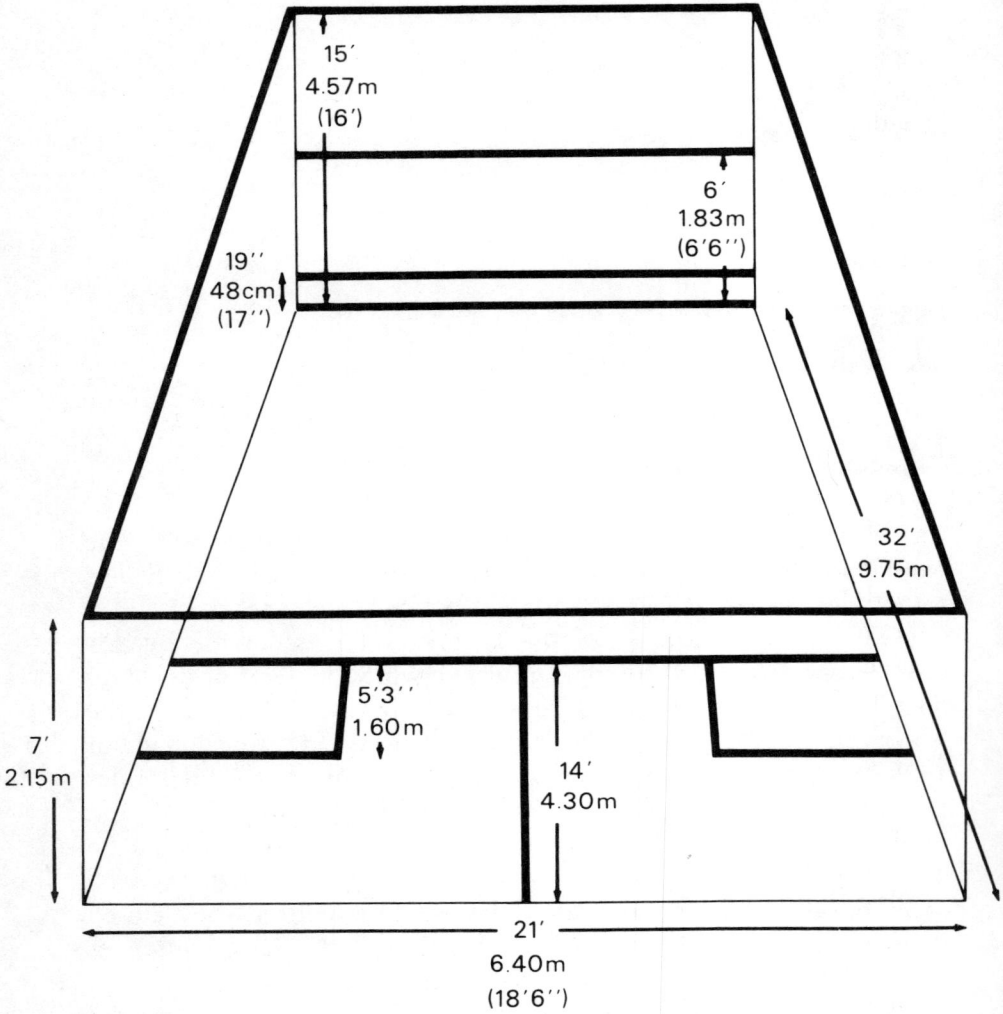

The International ("English") squash court.

Squash Racquets Federation and the United States Squash Racquets Association, lie in strengthening their ties, hence (despite denials), the introduction of the 70-plus ball, which is a step in that direction.

So how *does* the English game differ from a player's and spectator's point of view?

Since the ball moves more slowly, there is more time to run it down, and more work to be done before a big enough opening can be made to play a winning shot. Rallies tend to last longer, and there are a greater number of "high percentage" shots, as both players are reluctant to risk losing points that require so much labor to win. Conditioning becomes a factor in this, as the longer you can run, the later you need to take risks. In the English game there is much more room for the defensive player to force errors from opponents by persistence and physical attrition. At the same time, though, the extra period allowed for thought by a slower ball permits the tactical element in squash to be more obviously prominent, and allows brains frequently to triumph over brawn. This factor helps to integrate and extend the age range of effective players.

The size of the court makes more than two-and-a-half feet worth of difference to the game. It is quite impractical, for instance, to play a decent game with a 70-plus on an English court, since the ball travels far too fast to reach the extra space. The other way round—English ball on American court, is a popular summer game which helps many U.S. players tone up for the winter, but the ball just will not lie down. It's very hard to push anyone around with the English ball in a smaller space. Each court has evolved alongside a particular type of ball, and the differences in size, if not in idiosyncratic matters such as the shape of the sidewall and the service box, complement the characteristics of the balls. On an English court this means that the extra space gives a wider range for strokes and physical activity during longer rallies. The floor area of an English court is eighty square feet larger than that of the American. A winning shot is further hampered across the Atlantic by a tell-tale that is two inches higher. The serve, being crucial in the English game, becomes that much more difficult to make effective, owing to the sloping walls and the fact that a fault on the sidelines, as well as below the tell-tale and above the top front line, is a double fault.

The scoring system once again emphasizes the greater resilience and mental application required by this game. You may only win a point when "in hand" means that the serve can change hands a dozen times without a change in the score. Matches are thus stretched out.

Mentally, then, the keynote is discipline. One rule is to attack when serving, to take risks, but to defend when receiving. Make your opponent play, just make him play. If you lose the serve through taking risks, your opponent hasn't improved his position, just earned a serve. If you take a risk and lose when your opponent is serving, though, you're one-ninth closer to losing the game. The dilemma of when to take a risk has always seemed to be one of the charms of the English game that is absent from the American, where serving is often just beginning a point, and risks can as well be taken at any time as at any other.

Having said that discipline is the key, the actual formation of the strokes points the opposite way. Because of the greater amount of time available, which makes defense an easier proposition, attack must be as violent or as subtle as possible. The ball travels more slowly so it must be struck harder to reach the back or be killed with speed. The swing is therefore higher, longer, and more dramatic, and the sound of a full-blooded drive with an English ball can be electrifying.

The frequency of alley shots and crosscourts in the two games is similar, as is the importance of the "T." Despite the wider English court, it is difficult to generate enough pace on the crosscourt to safely pass a player standing anywhere near the "T." The differences arise in the frequency of strokes concerned with the front and back corners of the court. The drop shot, for instance, will stay closer to the front wall with an English ball, and is a means of creating openings as well as winning points. Although the attacking lob is often employed in America, the margin for error remains considerably smaller than in the English game. The boast, too, is now ubiquitous in 70-plus, to return the ball from the corners, to throw opponents the wrong way, but on the wider courts it may also be employed defensively to tax a player.

The English game is more physically demanding, though more fluent and less hurried than the American, where superiority tells more suddenly and the pace is hotter. In the American game certain qualities are more evident—fast reflexes, racquet skills, sudden controlled acceleration, accurate kills, single-mindedness; in the English game, conditioning, tenaciousness, flexibility, touch, court sense, and anticipation are stressed.

If you play the American game, there is considerable benefit to be derived from exposure to the English ball, if only on an American court. It will sharpen up your fitness, mobility, and tactical sense, if not your reflexes. You'll pick up a sense of perspective and see your 70-plus game more objectively. The two games are at least close enough for you to learn and play either and enjoy both.

16

CONCLUSION

Squash is a game of the future. The power in the North American game is moving firmly into the hands of big investors and entrepreneurs whose billings have yet to be made. If they continue to escalate promotion of the game, and break free of its more stolid traditions, anything can happen.

As you've probably already found, squash is an addictive game. There's something to grab everyone and hold them. The game has all the possibilities of tennis, but consumes less time and space; it has the accessibility of racquet-ball, its main rival, without being so dreadfully facile.

A sure sign of the arrival of squash is the treatment of its stars. They are beginning to have other people carry their kits, to ignore photographers, to arrive at clubs with groups of people waiting for them, to collect hefty checks for endorsing sports products. Women players are attracting the attention of cosmetic and fashion companies and women's magazines.

Probably the most important factor in the future of the game is the development of programs for young people. Until the current surge of growth, the private club/hardball heritage of the game in

Alicia McConnell, National "sixteen and under" champion, practices with her sister Patrice.

America militated against serious youthful interest in it. Competition and recognition were too limited among the few colleges and clubs that played, and the hardball, as well as requiring more patience at the beginning, did not put so large a premium on youth and vigor as does the 70-plus.

This situation has changed, in part as a result of the intelligence of some squash entrepreneurs who grasp that youth is the only secure foundation for their enterprises. However, there's a long way to go until age group leagues, local and national tournaments, like those in Australia or England, are established in America. Until this happens, continuity of interest in the game cannot be guaranteed, and the industry will live from day to day. If you like the game, encourage your children; in a few years, if they get to be champions, they'll be at the top of a very big sport.

The excitement of thousands of new players has transmitted itself to the administrators of the game; being around them is like waiting outside the delivery room. It is finally becoming clear that their game is perfectly tailored to the leisure requirements of millions of Americans.

Squash is growing as a spectator sport. It's one of those sports where the example of stars in action can inspire advances in your own game: "So *that's* how you do it."

If you want to see the big tournament pros and top amateurs, consult one of the crop of new publications covering squash— *Squash News, Squash Monthly, The Squash Player International,* or *Racquet*—all of which advertise and report tournaments. These used to be confined largely to the East Coast and Canada, but no longer. Probably your own club will be visited by top players from time to time, and if they aren't advertised, you can easily arrange with the staff to tip you off.

If you want to compete yourself, most clubs run ladders for different levels of competence, and hold at least annual tournaments for their men and women members. Group and corporate memberships at these clubs often start private ladders of their own. There are plenty of individual inter-club tournaments sponsored by firms such as Insilco, Slazenger, and Moody, again for all levels of player. Metropolitan team league competitions for men and women are run in many cities. Most of them are well organized and hotly contested by the three- or five-person club teams.

The range of competition is increasing almost as fast as it can be organized. Only when you compete seriously will you realize how important squash is to you. You'll be surprised how fast your game improves when you've got something to lose.

Having equipped yourself with the basic techniques and at least an idea of the rest, you have an exciting prospect—a lifetime of challenging recreation in a sport that is beginning its explosion.

APPENDIX I – DRILLS

The best way to practice squash is to play the game regularly with a partner—preferably a player of equal or superior proficiency. But while you're learning the fundamental strokes, the practice drills in this section can help you concentrate on one particular shot or technique. The first set of drills is intended for two players. Each drill allows both players to concentrate on a particular skill within the context of the game situation where that skill is used.

The remaining drills are intended for a single player alone on the court—and if you can't find a partner for your practice sessions, these drills will help sharpen your strokes. In the artificial situation of solo play, you can afford to take more time and really perfect your basic technique. But it's easier to be lazy and to lose continuity when you practice alone, so you'll have to work harder (and keep the game situation firmly in mind) to derive real benefit from this second set of drills.

DRILLS FOR TWO

Forehand/Backhand Alley Shot

The idea of this drill is to play a game in the rear forehand (or backhand) quadrant of the court. Score points as usual—but alter the boundaries. Once the ball is in play, any shot that bounces outside of the chosen quadrant is out of play. This drill will help you hit the alley shot to a good length on either forehand or backhand.

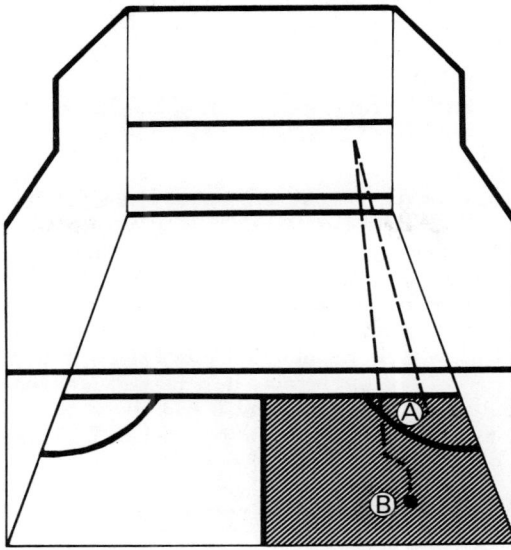

Footwork, Court Movement, Forehand and Backhand Alleys, Boasting from the Back

This looks like a complicated drill—but once mastered, it's probably the most rewarding. Player A hits the forehand alley shot toward the back corner, where B boasts it. A moves across to the front backhand corner to meet the boast, and plays a backhand alley shot. B then plays the backhand boast from the corner across to the forehand side. A then hits another forehand alley shot, and so on. A must remember to play a backhand when the ball bounces out of the front backhand corner, a forehand when it comes from the forehand corner. Player A's footwork and alley shots are tested under pressure, and player B must repeatedly play defensive boasts on both sides. After a bit of practice, this drill can continue indefinitely.

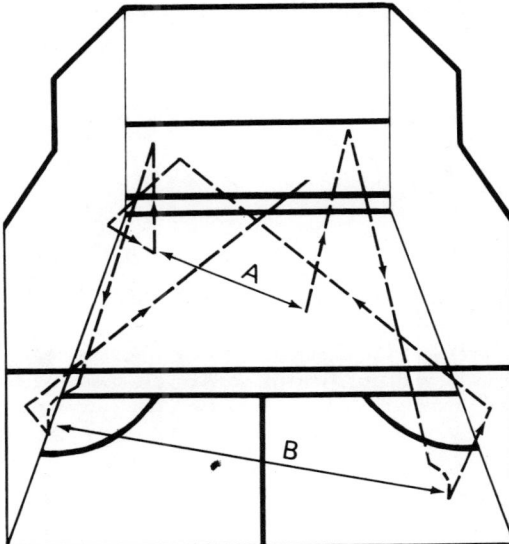

155

Forehand/Backhand Volleys from the "T," Defense from Deep Court

Player A begins this drill on the "T," player B begins in the forehand (or backhand) corner. A's objective is to retain position on the "T" (and confine B in the corner); B's objective is to take possession of the "T" by driving A into the corner with a well-placed alley shot. B hits the alley shot from the back corner, aiming to put the ball back into his corner. A moves across to intercept (usually with a volley), hitting the ball deep into B's corner, then returns to the "T." If A is successful in maintaining position on the "T," B must once again hit the alley shot into the corner. If A fails to intercept the alley shot, he'll have to move to the back corner, and B will take over position at the "T."

This drill imitates one of the commonest situations in the game; it is therefore a basic form of practice for two players.

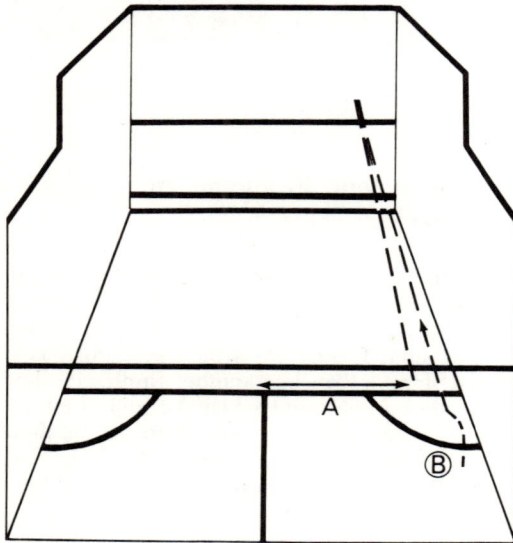

Lob, Drop, Boast, Lob Serve

This drill will not only improve a number of basic skills, but it will also train you to anticipate your opponent's next shot. A lobs crosscourt to B, who has the option of a drop shot or a boast. A, responding to B's shot, must quickly spot which it is, then lob crosscourt once again. As a variation, A may serve the lob from the forehand (or backhand) service box to begin each rally. This drill is about the only way for two players to practice touch shots with any continuity.

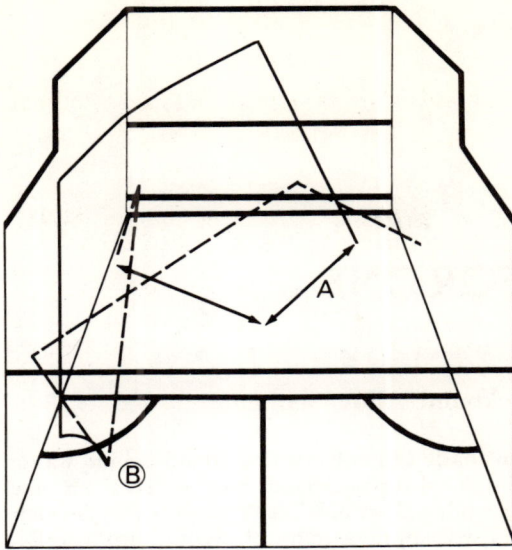

Crosscourts, Width Judgement

An interesting and useful game can be played by penalizing the player who doesn't hit his shot into the opposite rear quadrant. Score as usual. This drill will help improve the speed and accuracy of your crosscourt shot.

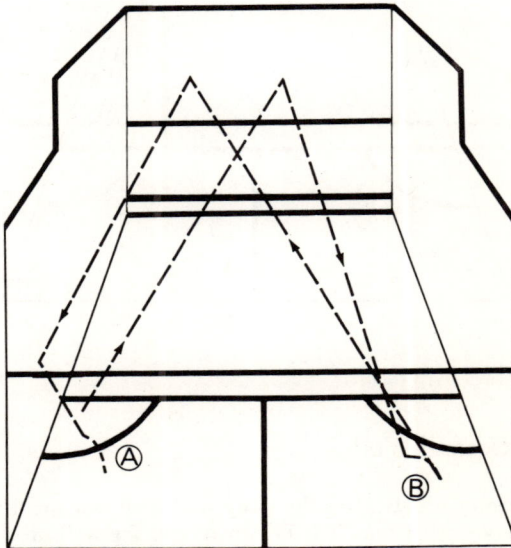

DRILLS FOR ONE

Forehand/Backhand Alley Shots

This is the most basic form of practice. Stand behind the service line and hit a succession of forehand (or backhand) alley shots. Each time, try to place the ball as close to the sidewall as possible. This drill will develop your consistency and accuracy, and will improve your ability to return a well-hit alley shot with another one.

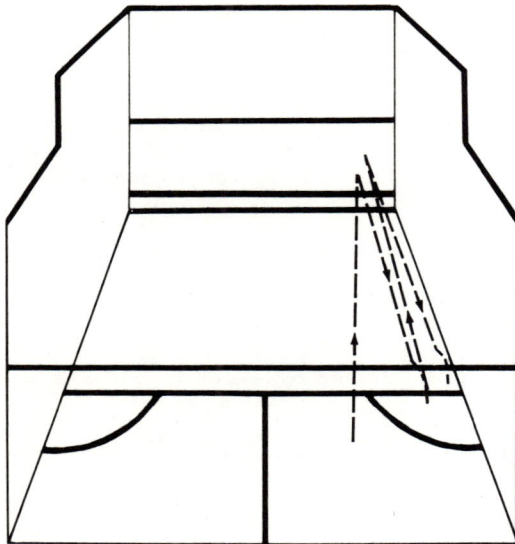

Forehand/Backhand Volleys

This drill is almost identical to the alley shot drill, except that you should be standing about level with the "T." Try to return the ball on the fly each time.

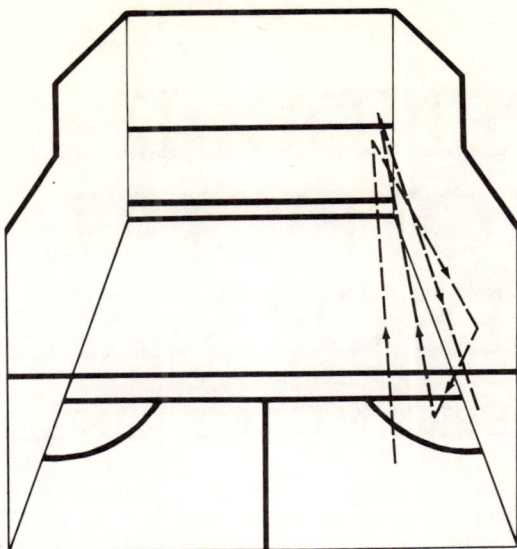

Drops and Boasts at the Front

Begin with a drop shot into the corner from the "T." Go after it, boast it across, play another drop, and boast back to the original corner. To practice just the attacking boast, simply leave out the drop shot.

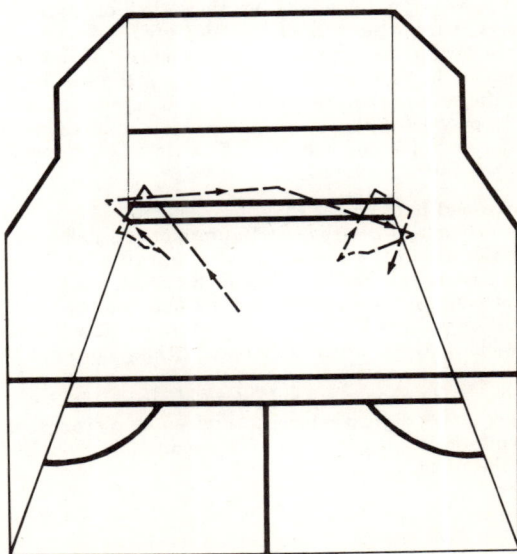

APPENDIX II – THE OFFICIAL RULES OF SQUASH

THE AMERICAN GAME (SINGLES)*

1. **Server.** At the start of a match the choice to serve or receive shall be decided by the spin of a racquet. The server retains the serve until he loses a point, in which event he loses the serve.

2. **Service.**

(a) The server, until the ball has left the racquet from the service, must stand with at least one foot on the floor within and not touching the line surrounding the service box and serve the ball onto the front wall above the service line and below the 16' line before it touches any other part of the court, so that on its rebound (return) it first strikes the floor within, but not touching, the lines of the opposite service court, either before or after touching any other wall or walls within the court. A ball so served is a good service, otherwise it is a Fault.

(b) If the first service is a Fault, the server shall serve again from the same side. If the server makes two consecutive Faults, he loses the point. A service called a Fault may not be played, but the receiver may volley any service which has struck the front wall in accordance with this rule.

(c) At the beginning of each game, and each time there is a new server, the ball shall be served by the winner of the previous point from whichever service box the server elects and thereafter alternately until the service is lost or until the end of the game. If the server serves from the wrong box there shall be no penalty and the service shall count as if served from the correct box, provided, however, that if the receiver does not attempt to return the service, he may demand that it be served from the other box, or if, before the receiver attempts to return the service, the Referee calls a Let (see Rule 9), the service shall be made from the other box.

(d) A ball is in play from the moment at which it is delivered in service until (1) the point is decided; (2) a Fault, as defined in 2(a) is made; or (3) a Let or Let Point occurs (See Rules 9 and 10).

3. **Return of Service and Subsequent Play.**

(a) A return is deemed to be made at the instant the ball touches the racquet of the player making the return. To make a good return of a service or of a subsequent return the ball must be struck on the volley or before it has touched the floor twice, and reach the front wall on the fly above the tell-tale and below the 16' line, and it may touch any wall or walls within the court before or after reaching the front wall. On any return the ball may be struck only once. It may not be "carried" or "double-hit."

(b) If the receiver fails to make a good return of a good service, the server wins the point. If the receiver makes a good return of service, the players shall alternate making returns until one player fails to make a good return. The player failing to make a good return loses the point.

---

* provided by the United States Squash Racquets Association.

(c) Until the ball has been touched or has hit the floor twice, it may be struck at any number of times.

(d) If at any time after a service the ball hits outside the playing surfaces of the court (the ceiling and/or lights, or on or above a line marking the perimeters of the playing surfaces of the court), the player so hitting the ball loses the point, unless a Let or a Let Point occurs. (See Rules 9 and 10.)

4. **Score.** Each point won by a player shall add one to his score.

5. **Game.** The player who first scores fifteen points wins the game excepting that:

(a) At "thirteen all" the player who has first reached the score of thirteen must elect one of the following before the next serve:

(1) Set to five points—making the game eighteen points.
(2) Set to three points—making the game sixteen points.
(3) No set, in which event the game remains fifteen points.

(b) At "fourteen all"—provided the score has not been "thirteen all"—the player who has first reached the score of fourteen must elect one of the following before the next serve:

(1) Set to three points—making the game seventeen points.
(2) No set, in which event the game remains fifteen points.

6. **Match.** The player who first wins three games wins the match, except that a player may be awarded the match at any time upon the retirement, default or disqualification of an opponent.

7. **Right to Play Ball.** Immediately after striking the ball a player must get out of an opponent's way and must:

(a) Give an opponent a fair view of the ball, provided, however, interference purely with an opponent's vision in following the flight of the ball is not a Let (See Rule 9).

(b) Give an opponent a fair opportunity to get to and/or strike at the ball in and from any position on the court elected by the opponent; and

(c) Allow an opponent to play the ball to any part of the front wall or to either side wall near the front wall.

8. **Ball in Play Touching Player.**

(a) If a ball in play, after hitting the front wall, but before being returned again, shall touch either player, or anything he wears or carries (other than the racquet of the player who makes the return) the player so touched loses the point, except as provided in Rule 9(a) or 9(b).

(b) If a ball in play touches the player who last returned it or anything he wears or carries before it hits the front wall, the player so touched loses the point.

(c) If a ball in play, after being struck by a player on a return, hits the player's opponent or anything the opponent wears or carries before reaching the front wall:

(1) The player who made the return shall lose the point if the return would not have been good.

(2) The player who made the return shall win the point if the ball, except for such interference, would have hit the front wall fairly; provided, however, the point shall be a Let (see Rule 9) if:

(i) The ball would have touched some other wall before so hitting the front wall.

(ii) The ball has hit some other wall before hitting the player's opponent or anything he wears or carries.

(iii) The player who made the return shall have turned following the ball around prior to playing the ball.

(d) If a player strikes at and misses the ball, he may make further attempts to return it. If, after being missed, the ball touches his opponent or anything he wears or carries:

(1) If the player might otherwise have made a good return, the point shall be a Let.

(2) If the player could not have made a good return, he shall lose the point.

If any further attempt is successful but the ball, before reaching the front wall, touches his opponent or anything he wears or carries and Rule 8(c)(2) applies, the point shall be a Let.

(e) When there is no referee, if the player who made the return does not concede that the return would not have been good, or, alternatively, the player's opponent does not concede that the ball has hit him (or anything he wears or carries) and would have gone directly to the front wall without first touching any other wall, the point shall be a Let.

(f) When there is no referee, if the players are unable to agree whether 8(d)(1) or 8(d)(2) applies, the point shall be a Let.

9. Let. A let is the playing over of a point.

On the replay of the point the server (1) is entitled to two serves even if a Fault was called on the original point, (2) must serve from the correct box even if he served from the wrong box on the original point, and (3) provided he is a new server, may serve from a service box other than the one selected on the original point.

In addition to the Lets described in Rules 2(c) and 8(c), the following are Lets if the player whose turn it is to strike the ball could otherwise have made a good return:

(a) When such player's opponent violates Rule 7.

(b) When owing to the position of such player, his opponent is unable to avoid being touched by the ball.

(c) When such player refrains from striking at the ball because of a reasonable fear of injuring his opponent.

(d) When such player before or during the act of striking or striking at the ball is touched by his opponent, his racquet or anything he wears or carries.

(e) When on the first bounce from the floor the ball hits on or above the six and one half foot line on the back wall; and

(f) When a ball in play breaks. If a player thinks the ball has broken while play is in progress he must nevertheless complete the point and then immediately request a Let, giving the ball to the Referee for inspection. The Referee shall allow a Let only upon such immediate request if the ball in fact proves to be broken (See Rule 13(c)).

A player may request a Let or a Let Point (See Rule 10). A request by a player for a Let shall automatically include a request for a Let Point. Upon such request, the Referee shall allow a Let, Let Point or no Let.

No Let shall be allowed on any stroke a player makes unless he requests such before or during the act of striking or striking at the Ball.

The Referee may not call or allow a Let as defined in this Rule 9 unless such Let is requested by a player; provided, however, the Referee may call a Let at any time (1) when there is interference with play caused by any factor beyond the control of the players, or (2) when he fears that a player is about to suffer severe physical injury.

10. Let Point. A Let Point is the awarding of a point to a player when an opponent unnecessarily violates Rule 7(b) or 7(c).

An unnecessary violation occurs (1) when the player fails to make the necessary effort within the scope of his normal ability to avoid the violation, thereby depriving his opponent of a clear opportunity to attempt a winning shot, or (2) when the player has repeatedly failed to make the necessary effort within the scope of his normal ability to avoid such violations.

The Referee may not award a Let Point as defined in this Rule 10 unless such a Let Point or a Let (see Rule 9) is requested by a player.

When there is no referee, if a player does not concede that he has unnecessarily violated Rule 7(b) or 7(c), the point shall be a Let.

11. Continuity of Play. Play shall be continuous from the first service of each game until the game is concluded. Play shall never be suspended solely to allow a player to recover his strength or wind. The provisions of this Rule 11 shall be strictly construed. The Referee shall be the sole judge of intentional delay, and, after giving due warning, he must default the offender.

Between each game play may be suspended by either player for a period not to exceed two minutes. Between the third and fourth games play may be suspended by either player for a period not to exceed five minutes. Except during the five minute period at the end of the third game, no player may leave the court without permission of the referee.

Except as otherwise specified in this Rule 11, the Referee may suspend play for such reason and for such period of time as he may consider necessary.

If play is suspended by the Referee because of injury to one of the players, such player must resume play within one hour from the point and game score existing at the time play was suspended or default the match, provided, however, if a player suffers cramps or pulled muscles, play may be suspended by the Referee once during a match for such player for a period not to exceed five minutes after which time such player must resume play or default the match.

In the event the Referee suspends play other than for injury to a player, play shall be resumed when the Referee determines the cause of such suspension of play has been eliminated, provided, however, if such cause of delay cannot be rectified within one hour, the match shall be postponed to such time as the Tournament Committee determines. Any such suspended match shall be resumed from the point and game score existing at the time the match was stopped unless the Referee and both players unanimously agree to play the entire match or any part of it over.

12. Attire and Equipment.

(a) The color of a player's shirt or trousers may be either white or a solid pastel. The Referee's decision as to a player's attire shall be final.

(b) A standard singles ball as specified in the Court, Racquet and Ball Specifications of this Association shall be used.

(c) A racquet as specified in the Court, Racquet and Ball Specifications of this Association shall be used.

13. Condition of Ball.

(a) No ball, before or during a match, may be artificially treated, that is, heated or chilled.

(b) At any time, when not in the actual play of a point, another ball may be substituted by the mutual consent of the players or by decision of the Referee.

(c) A ball shall be determined broken when it has a crack which extends through both its inner and outer surfaces. The ball may be squeezed only enough to determine the extent of the crack. A broken ball shall be replaced and the preceding point shall be a Let (See Rule 9(f)).

(d) A cracked (but not broken) ball may be replaced by the mutual consent of the players or by decision of the Referee, and the preceding point shall stand.

14. Court.

(a) The singles court shall be as specified in the Court, Racquet and Ball Specifications of this Association.

(b) No equipment of any sort shall be permitted to remain in the court during a match other than the ball used in play, the racquets being used by the players, and the clothes worn by them. All other equipment, such as extra balls, extra racquets, sweaters when not being worn, towels, bathrobes, etc., must be left outside the court. A player who requires a towel or cloth to wipe himself or anything he wears or carries should keep same in his pocket or securely fastened to his belt or waist.

15. Referee.

(a) A Referee shall control the game. This control shall be exercised from time the players enter the court. The Referee may limit the time of the warm up period to five minutes, or shall terminate a longer warm up period so that the match commences at the scheduled time.

(b) The Referee's decision on all questions of play shall be final except as provided in Rule 15(c).

(c) Two judges may be appointed to act on any appeal by a player to a decision of the Referee. When such judges are acting in a match, a player may appeal any decision of the Referee to the judges, except a decision under Rules 11, 12(a), 13, 15(a) and 15(f). If one judge agrees with the Referee, the Referee's decision stands; if both judges disagree with the Referee, the judges' decision is final. The judges shall make no ruling unless an appeal has been made. The decision of the judges shall be announced promptly by the Referee.

(d) A player may not request the removal or replacement of the Referee or a judge during a match.

(e) A player shall not state his reason for his request under Rule 9 for a Let or Let Point or for his appeal from any decision of the Referee provided, however, that the Referee may request the player to state his reasons.

(f) A Referee serving without judges, after giving due warning of the penalty of this Rule 15(f), in his discretion may disqualify a player for speech or conduct unbecoming to the game of squash racquets, provided that a player may be disqualified without warning if, in the opinion of such Referee, he has deliberately caused physical injury to his opponent.

When two judges are acting in a match, the Referee in his discretion, upon the agreement of both judges, may disqualify a player with or without prior warning for speech or conduct unbecoming to the game of squash racquets.

THE INTERNATIONAL GAME (SINGLES)*

DEFINITIONS.

Board. The expression denoting a line, the top edge of which is 19 inches (.483m.) from the floor, set out upon the upper edge of a band of resonant material fixed upon the front wall and extending the full width of the court.

Cut Line. A line set out upon the front wall, six feet (1.829m.) above the floor and extending the full width of the court.

Game Ball. The state of the game when the server requires one point to win is said to be "Game Ball".

Half-Court Line. A line set out upon the floor parallel to the sidewalls, dividing the back half of the court into two equal parts called right half court and left half court respectively.

Hand-in. The player who serves.

Hand-out. The player who receives the service.

Hand. The period from the time when a player becomes hand-in until he becomes hand-out.

Not-up. The expression used to denote that a ball has not been returned above the board in accordance with the rules.

Out of Court. The ball is out of court when it touches the front, sides or back of the court above the area prepared for play or passes over any cross bars or other part of the roof of the court. The lines delimiting such area, the lighting equipment and the roof are out of court.

Service Box or Box. A delimited area in each half of court from within which hand-in serves.

Short Line. A line set out upon the floor parallel to and 18 feet (5.486m.) from the front wall and extending the full width of the court.

Striker. The player whose turn it is to play after the ball has hit the front wall.

Time or Stop. Expression used by the referee to stop play.

---

* as approved by the International Squash Rackets Federation.

1. **The Game.** The game of squash rackets is played between two players with standard rackets, with balls bearing the standard mark of the S.R.A. and in a rectangular court of standard dimensions enclosed on all four sides.

2. **The Score.** A match shall consist of the best of three or five games at the option of the promoters of the competition. Each game is 9 up: that is to say the player who first wins 9 points wins the game except that, on the score being called 8-all for the first time, hand-out may, if he chooses, before the next service is delivered, set the game to 2, in which case the player who first scores two more points wins the game. Hand-out must in either case clearly indicate his choice to the marker, if any, and to his opponent.[1]

3. **Scoring.** Points can only be scored by hand-in. When a player fails to serve or to make a good return in accordance with the rules, his opponent wins the stroke. When hand-in wins a stroke, he scores a point; when hand-out wins a stroke, he becomes hand-in.

4. **The Right to Serve.** The right to serve first is decided by the spin of a racket. Thereafter the server continues to serve until he loses a stroke, when his opponent becomes the server, and so on throughout the match.

5. **Service.** The ball before being struck shall be thrown in the air and shall not touch the walls or floor. The ball shall be served on to the front wall so that on its return, unless volleyed, it would fall to the floor in the quarter court nearest the back wall and opposite to the server's box from which the service has been delivered.

At the beginning of each game and of each hand, the server may serve from either box, but after scoring a point he shall then serve from the other and so on alternately as long as he remains hand-in or until the end of the game. If the server serves from the wrong box there shall be no penalty and the service shall count as if served from the right box, except that hand-out may, if he does not attempt to take the service, demand that it be served from the other box.

6. **Good Service.** A service is good which is not a fault or which does not result in the server serving his hand out in accordance with rule 9. If the server serves one fault he shall serve again.

7. **Fault.** A service is a fault (unless the server serves his hand out under rule 9):
   (a) If the server fails to stand with one foot at least within and not touching the line surrounding the service box (called a foot fault);
   (b) If the ball is served on to or below the cut line;
   (c) If the ball served first touches the floor on or in front of the short line;
   (d) If the ball served first touches the floor in the wrong half court or on the half-court line.
   (The wrong half court is the left for a service from the left-hand box and the right for a service from the right-hand box.)

8. **Fault, If Taken.** Hand-out may take a fault. If he attempts to do so, the service thereupon becomes good and the ball continues in play. If he does not attempt to do so, the ball shall cease to be in play provided that, if the ball, before it has bounced twice upon the floor, touches the server or anything he wears or carries, the server shall lose the stroke.

9. **Serving Hand-Out.** The server serves his hand-out and loses the stroke.
   (a) If the ball is served on to or below the board or out of court or against any part of the court before the front wall;
   (b) If he fails to strike the ball or strikes the ball more than once;
   (c) If he serves two consecutive faults.
   (d) If the ball before it has bounced twice upon the floor, or has been struck by his opponent touches the server or anything he wears or carries.

---

[1] *Note to referees.* If hand-out does not make clear his choice before the next service, the referee shall stop play and require him to do so.

10. **Let.** A let is an undecided stroke and the service or rally in respect of which a let is allowed shall not count and the server shall serve again from the same box. A let shall not annul a previous fault.

11. **The Play.** After a good service has been delivered the players return the ball alternately until one or other fails to make a good return or the ball otherwise ceases to be in play in accordance with the rules.

12. **Good Return.** A return is good if the ball, before it has bounced twice upon the floor, is returned by the striker on to the front wall above the board without touching the floor or any part of the striker's body or clothing, provided the ball is not hit twice or out of court.[2]

13. **Strokes, How Won.** A player wins a stroke:

    (a) Under rule 9;

    (b) If his opponent fails to make a good return of the ball in play;

    (c) If the ball in play touches the striker or his opponent or anything he wears or carries, except as is otherwise provided by rules 14 and 15.

14. **Hitting An Opponent With the Ball.** If an otherwise good return of the ball has been made, but before reaching the front wall it hits the striker's opponent or his racket or anything he wears or carries, then:

    (a) If the ball would have made a good return and would have struck the front wall without first touching any other wall, the striker shall win the stroke, except that, if the striker shall have followed the ball round and so turned before making a stroke, a let shall be allowed;

    (b) If the ball would otherwise have made a good return, a let shall be allowed;

    (c) If the ball would not have made a good return, the striker shall lose the stroke.

The ball shall cease to be in play, even if it subsequently goes up.

15. **Further Attempts to Hit the Ball.** If the striker strikes at and misses the ball, he may make further attempts to return it. If after being missed, the ball accidentally touches his opponent or his racket or anything he wears or carries, then:

    (a) If the striker could otherwise have made a good return, a let shall be allowed;

    (b) If the striker could not have made a good return he loses the stroke.

If any such further attempt is successful but the ball before reaching the front wall hits the striker's opponent or his racket or anything he wears or carries, a let shall be allowed and rule 14 (a) shall not apply.

16. **Appeals.** An appeal may be made against any decision of the marker.

    (i) The following rules shall apply to appeals on the service:

        (a) No appeal shall be made in respect of foot faults.

        (b) No appeal shall be made in respect of the marker's call of "fault" to the first service.

        (c) If the marker calls "fault" to the second service, the server may appeal and, if the decision is reversed, a let shall be allowed.

        (d) If the marker does not call "fault" or "out of court" to the second service, hand-out may appeal even if he attempts to take the ball, and if the decision is reversed, hand-out becomes hand-in.

        (e) If the marker does not call "fault" or "out of court" to the first service, hand-out may appeal if he makes no attempt to take the ball. If the appeal is disallowed, hand-out shall lose the stroke.

    (ii) An appeal under rule 12 or 16 (i) (d) shall be made at the end of the rally in which the stroke in dispute has been played.

---

[2] *Note to referees.* It shall not be considered a good return if the ball touches the board either before or after it hits the front wall.

(iii) In all cases where an appeal for a let is desired, this appeal shall be made by addressing the referee with the words "Let, please". Play shall thereupon cease until the referee has given his decision.

(iv) No appeal may be made after the delivery of a service for anything that occurred before that service was delivered.

17. Fair View and Freedom of Stroke.

(i) After making a stroke a player must get out of his opponent's way as much as possible. If, in the opinion of the referee, a player has not made every effort to do this the referee shall stop play and award a stroke to his opponent.

(ii) When a player:
(a) fails to give his opponent a fair view of the ball,
(Note: a player shall be considered to have had a fair view unless the ball returns too close to his opponent for the player to sight it adequately for the purpose of making a stroke;)
(b) fails to avoid interfering with, or crowding his opponent in getting to or striking at the ball,
(c) fails to allow his opponent, as far as his opponent's position allows him, freedom to play the ball to any part of the front wall and to either side wall near the front wall, the referee may on appeal or without waiting for an appeal allow a let; but if in the opinion of the referee a player has not made every effort to comply with these requirements of the rule, the referee shall stop play and award a stroke to his opponent.

Notwithstanding anything contained above, if a player suffers interference from or distraction by his opponent, and in the opinion of the referee, is thus prevented from making a winning return, he shall be awarded the stroke.[3]

18. Let, When Allowed. Notwithstanding anything contained in these rules.

(i) A let may be allowed:
(a) If, owing to the position of the striker, his opponent is unable to avoid being touched by the ball before the return is made; [4]
(b) If the ball in play touches any article lying in the court;
(c) If the player refrains from hitting the ball owing to a reasonable fear of injuring his opponent;
(d) If the player in the act of striking touches his opponent;
(e) If the referee is asked to decide an appeal and is unable to do so;
(f) If the player drops his racket, calls out or in any other way distracts the attention of his opponent and the referee considers such occurrence to have caused his opponent to lose the stroke.

(ii) A let shall be allowed:
(a) If hand-out is not ready and does not attempt to take the service;
(b) If a ball breaks during play;
(c) If an otherwise good return has been made, but the ball goes out of court on its first bounce;

---

[3] *Notes to referees.* (a) The practice of impeding an opponent's strokes by crowding or by obscuring his view is highly detrimental to the game and referees should have no hesitation in enforcing the penultimate paragraph of this rule. (b) The words "interfering with . . . his opponent in getting to . . . the ball" must be interpreted so as to include the case of a player having to wait for an excessive swing of his opponent's racket.

[4] *Note to referees.* This rule shall be construed to include the cases of the striker whose position in front of his opponent makes it impossible for the latter to see the ball or who shapes as if to play the ball and changes his mind at the last moment preferring to take the ball off the back wall, the ball in either case hitting the opponent who is between the striker and the back wall. This is not, however, to be taken as conflicting in any way with the referee's duties under rule 17.

(d) As provided for by rules 14, 15, 16 (i) (c) and 22.

(iii) Provided always that no let shall be allowed:

    (a) In respect of any stroke which a player attempts to make unless in making the stroke he touches his opponent; except as provided for under rules 18 (ii) (b) and (c) and 15.

    (b) Unless the striker could have made a good return.

(iv) Unless an appeal is made by one of the players, no let shall be allowed except where these rules definitely provide for a let, namely rules 14 (a), 14 (b) and 17 and paragraphs (ii) (b) and (c) of rule 18.

19. New Ball. At any time when the ball is not in actual play a new ball may be substituted by mutual consent of the players or on appeal by either player at the discretion of the referee.

20. Knock-ups.[5] The referee shall allow to either player or to the two players together a period of five minutes during the hour preceding the start of a match for knocking up in a court in which a match is to be played. The choice of knocking up first shall be decided by the spin of a racket.

21. Play in a Match is to be Continuous. After the first service is delivered, play shall be continuous so far as is practical, provided that at any time play may be suspended owing to bad light or other circumstances beyond the control of the players for such period as the referee shall decide. The referee shall award the match to the opponent of any player who, in his opinion, persists, after due warning, in delaying the play in order to recover his strength or wind, or for any other reason. However, an interval of one minute shall be permitted between games and of two minutes between the fourth and fifth games of a five-game match. A player may leave the court during such intervals, but shall be ready to resume play at the end of the stated time. Should he fail to do so when required by the referee the match shall be awarded to his opponent. In the event of play being suspended for the day, the match shall start afresh, unless both players agree to the contrary.[6]

22. Duties of Marker. The game is controlled by the marker, who shall call the play and the score. The server's score is called first. He shall call "Fault" (Rule 7 (b), (c) and (d)), "Foot Fault" (rule 7(a)), "Out of Court" or "Not Up" as the case may be. If in the course of play the marker calls "not up" or "out of court" the rally shall cease. If the marker's decision is reversed on appeal a "let" shall be allowed except that if the marker fails to call a ball "not up" or "out of court", and on appeal, it is ruled that such was in fact the case, the stroke shall be awarded accordingly.

Any return shall be considered good unless otherwise called.

If after the server has served one fault a "let" is allowed, the marker shall call "one fault" before the server serves again.

When no referee is appointed, the marker shall exercise all the powers of the referee.

23. The Referee. A referee may be appointed, to whom all appeals shall be directed, including appeals from the marker's decisions and calls. He shall not normally interfere with the marker's calling of the game except:

    (a) upon appeal by one of the players;

    (b) as provided for in rule 17;

    (c) when it is apparent to him that the marker has made a mistake in calling the game.

Notwithstanding the above, in the absence of an appeal, if it is evident that the score has been called incorrectly, the referee shall draw the marker's attention to this fact.

When a decision has been made by the referee, he shall announce it to the players,

---

[5] *Editor's Note.* Read "warm-up" for the English term "knock-up."

[6] *Note to referees.* A player may not open the door or leave the court other than between games with the referee's permission.

and the marker shall repeat it with the consequent score, e.g. "let ball", "no let" or "point to—."

24. **Power of Referee in Exceptional Cases.** The referee has power to order:

   (a) A player who has left the court to play on;

   (b) A player to leave the court for any reason whatsoever and to award the match to his opponent;

   (c) A match to be awarded to a player whose opponent fails to be present in the court within ten minutes of the advertised time of play.

   (d) Play to be stopped in order that a player or players may be warned that their conduct on the court is leading to an infringement of the rules.[7]

25. **Colour of Players Clothing.** Players are required to wear white clothing. The referee's decision thereon to be final.

---

[7] *Note to referee.* A referee should avail himself of this rule as early as possible where one or the other of the players is showing a tendency to break the provisions of rule 17.

APPENDIX III – PLACES TO PLAY

SQUASH FACILITIES IN THE UNITED STATES: 1977

Symbols used

1S = 1 regulation singles
1D = 1 regulation doubles
1E = 1 English dimensions
† = Transients welcome
* = Off-size court, frequently handball with removable tell-tale

ALABAMA
Gunter Air Force Base 1S

ALASKA
Anchorage
Elmendorf Air Force Base 1S, 1D
Fairbanks
private court 1S*

ARIZONA
Fort Huachuca—Special Services 2S*
Luke Air Force Base 1S

Phoenix
†Phoenix Downtown YMCA 1S*
Tucson
†L. A. Lohse Branch YMCA 1S*
South Branch (YMCA) 1S*

ARKANSAS
Little Rock
Little Rock YMCA 2S
Warren
Warren YMCA 2S*

CALIFORNIA
Alameda
Alameda Naval Air Station 1S
Bakersfield
Kern County YMCA 1S*
Barstow
Marine Corps Logistics Support Base 1S*

Berkeley
Univ. of California Squash
  Racquets Club 5S
Carmel
private court 1S
Carpinteria
Cate School 2S
Castle Air Force Base 1S
Chico
Chico State 6S, 2D
Claremont
Claremont Men's College 1S
Concord
Naval Weapons Station 2S*
Davis
University of California 2S
Edwards Air Force Base 1S
Escondido
private court 1S
Fairfield
Travis Air Force Base 1S
†*Fort Ord* 1S*
Foster City
Wallbangers Court Centers 1S
Fresno
†Central Valley YMCA 2S
  Fig Garden Swim & Racquets Club 2S
  Fresno YMCA 2S
  San Joaquin Athletic & Racquet
    Club 2S
Glendale
Glendale YMCA 1S*
Irvine
Orange Squash & Racquet Club 1S
La Canada
Crescenta Canada YMCA 1S*
La Jolla
Scripps Clinic, La Jolla 1S
Scripps Clinic, No. Torrey Pines Rd. . 1S
Scripps Clinic, South Coast Blvd. 1S
Univ. of Cal.—San Diego 1S, 1S*
Lemoore
Naval Air Station 2S*
Long Beach
Downtown Branch (YMCA) 1S*
Naval Support Activity, Special
  Services 4S
Pacific Coast Club 1S, 1S*
Los Alamitos
Los Alamitos Naval Air Station 3S
Los Altos
Los Altos Executive Club 1S
Los Angeles
Century West Club 1S
Hollywood YMCA 1S*

†Los Angeles Athletic Club 1S
  U.C.L.A. 1S
  University Club of Los Angeles 3S
  U.S.C. 1S*
  Westchester (L.A.) YMCA 2S*
  Westside J.C.C. 1S, 1S*
†*March A.F.B.* 1S*
Moffett Field
Naval Air Station 2S
Monterey
†Naval Post Graduate School 2S
†Pacheco Club 2S*
North Island NAS 1S, 1D
Novato
Hamilton A.F.B. Squash Club 1S
Oakland
Naval Supply Center 2S
Orinda
private courts 4S
private court 1S*
Pasadena
Pasadena Athletic Club 1S*
†Pasadena YMCA—Downtown
  Branch 2S
Point Mugu
Naval Air Station 2S
Pomona
Pomona YMCA 1S*
Rancho Mirage
Mission Hills Country Club 2S
Redlands
Redlands YMCA 2S*
San Bernardino
San Bernardino YMCA 2S*
private court 1S*
San Diego
Com. Sub. Pac. Rep.—USN,
  Ballast Point 1S*
Cuyamaca Club 2S
Marine Recruit Center (N.T.C.) 1S
Naval Training Center 3S
Navy Athletic Field 1S
North Island Naval Air Station 2S
San Carlos Swim and Racquet
  Club 2S
San Francisco
†Anderson Air Force Base 2S*
Bay Racquet Club 3S
J.C.C. 1S
†Naval Submarine Base 1S
Olympic Club 2S, 1S*
Pacific Union Club 1S*
Presidio 1S, 2S*
†San Francisco Central YMCA 1S, 2S*
San Francisco Racquet Club 2S
University of California Medical
  Center 2S

†University Club of San
  Francisco   4S, 1D

San Luis Obispo
California State Polytechnic   6S, 6S*

San Mateo
†Peninsula Squash Club   4S

Santa Monica
Santa Monica YMCA   1S*

Sonoma
NSGA–Special Services   1S*

Stanford
Stanford University   4S

Sunnyvale
Supreme Court 1   1S

Torrance
El Camino College   1S
†South Bay Squash Racquets Club 2S

Venice
Venice Squash Club   3S

Victorville
George AFB   1S*

Watsonville
Cabrillo College   9S

COLORADO

Aspen
†Aspen Athletic Club   1S

Boulder
†Rallysport–Boulder   1S
University of Colorado   2S

Colorado Springs
Broadmoor Hotel Golf Club 1S, 2S*
Colorado College   2S
Ent AFB   4S
Fountain Valley School   2S
†Pikes Peak-Y/USO   1S, 1S*
U.S. Air Force Academy 20S, 3D

Denver
Air Force Accounting and
  Finance Center   1S
†Central YMCA   2S
Denver Athletic Club   3S, 1D
†The Denver Club   2S, 1D
Gates Rubber Co.   2S, 1D
†Jewish Community Center   1S
University Club-Denver 1S, 1D

Glendale
Executive Tower Inn Athletic
  Club   1S
Glendale YMCA   1S*
private courts   3S
†*Lowry AFB*   3S*

CONNECTICUT

Ansonia
Ansonia YMCA   1S*

Bridgeport

Bridgeport Branch (YMCA) 2S*
University Club   2S*

Farmington
private courts   2S

Greenwich
Field Club of Greenwich 2S, 1D
Greenwich Country Club 2S, 1D
private court   1S, 1D

Hartford
Aetna Life and Casualty 2S, 1D
Hartford YMCA   2S
Institute of Living   1S
Trinity College   6S

Kent
Kent School   3S

Litchfield
Forman School   1S

Middletown
Wesleyan University   14S, 1D

New Britain
†New Britain YMCA   2S

New Canaan
Country Club of New Canaan 1S
New Canaan YMCA   1S, 2S*
private court   1S*

New Haven
New Haven Lawn Club   5S
New Haven YMCA   2S*
Quinnipiack Club   2S
Yale University   35S, 2D

New London
Connecticut College   1S
New London YMCA   1S*

New Milford
Canterbury School   2S*

Norfolk
private court   1S

Norwich
Norwich YMCA   2S*

Pomfret
Pomfret School   4S

Sharon
private court   1S

Simsbury
Westminster School   3S*

Storrs
University of Connecticut 8S

Wallingford
Choate-Rosemary Hall School 10S

Waterbury
Waterbury YMCA   1S*

Watertown
Taft School   2S

West Hartford
Hartford Community Center 1S
Hartford Golf Club   4S

Hartford Jewish Community
Center   2S

DELAWARE
Dover Air Force Base   2S
Middletown
St. Andrew's School   4S
Newark
University of Delaware   2S, 10S*
Wilmington
Tower Hill School   4S, 1D
†Wilmington Central YMCA   3S
Wilmington Country Club   4S, 2D
†Wilmington Racquets Club,
Inc.   4S, 1D

DISTRICT OF COLUMBIA
Andrews Air Force Base   2S
Bolling AFB   3S
†Central YMCA   4S
Georgetown University   1S
George Washington University   2S
Metropolitan Club   2S
Officers' Athletic Center—
The Pentagon   5S
University Club   4S

FLORIDA
Boca Raton
†YMCA of Boca Raton   1S
Fort Lauderdale
Fort Lauderdale Athletic Club   2S*
†The Players Club   4S, 1D
The Tennis Club   2S
Jacksonville
†NAS–Cecil Field   2S*
†Sports Complex, Inc.   1S
University Club   2S
Key West
Naval Air Station   2S*
Patrick Air Force Base   2S
Pensacola
†NAS–Pensacola   2S*
NTTC Corry Station   1S
St. Augustine
Valencia   1S*
Sarasota
Sarasota YMCA   1S
Tampa
MacDill A.F.B.   1S
Tower Club   1S*
Tampa YMCA   1S*

GEORGIA
Albany
Albany YMCA   1S
Americus
Georgia Southwestern   4S*

Athens
†Navy Supply Corps School   1D
Atlanta
Atlanta Athletic Club   2S
C & S Bank   2S
Capital City Club   2S
Emory University   1S*
Northside Branch (YMCA)   1S*
Piedmont Driving Club   3S, 1D
Terminus International Tennis
Club   1S
Tower H.C.   1S
YMCA   2S*
Augusta
Richmond Hotel Health Club   1S
Big Canoe
Big Canoe Racquet Center   1S
Decatur
Fairington Golf & Tennis   1S
Fort Benning   2S
Marietta
†Naval Air Station   1D
Mount Vernon
Brewton-Parker   2S*
Robins AFB   2S
Savannah
Savannah YMCA   2S*
Valdosta
Moody AFB   1S*
Valdosta State   4S, 4S*

HAWAII
Barber's Point
Naval Air Station   1S
Hickman AFB   1S
Honolulu
†Central Branch YMCA   1S*
Laie
Church College of Hawaii   1S*
Pearl Harbor
U.S. Naval Submarine Base   1S

IDAHO
Boise
†Boise Family YMCA   1S
Mountain Home
Mountain Home A.F.B.   1S

ILLINOIS
Aurora
Aurora YMCA   1S*
Champaign
University of Illinois   7S
Chicago
Austin "Y"   1S*
Chicago Athletic Ass'n.   3S
Chicago Club   1S

Downtown Court Club	2S		Lafayette	
Illinois Athletic Club	1S, 1S*		Purdue University	14S
Lake Shore Club	3S		**Michigan City**	
†Lawson YMCA	3S		Sullair Squash & Smash Club	1D
Racquet Club of Chicago	2S, 2D		**Muncie**	
Sears Roebuck YMCA	1S, 3S*		Muncie YMCA	1S*
Union League Club of Chicago	2S		**Notre Dame**	
University Club	5S, 1D		University of Notre Dame	6S
University of Illinois (Circle Campus)	5S*, 1D		**Portland** private court	1S
Women's Athletic Club	1S		**Terre Haute**	
Decatur			Terre Haute YMCA	2S*
Decatur YMCA	1S			
Des Plaines			**IOWA**	
Northwest Suburban YMCA	2S*		**Cedar Rapids**	
Elsah			†Cedar Rapids Central YMCA	1S
Principia College	1S, 1D		**Davenport**	
Great Lakes			Davenport Family "Y"	2S
Special Services Dep't.	2S*		**Des Moines**	
Joliet			†Des Moines Central YMCA	2S
Joliet YMCA	1S*		**Keokuk**	
La Grange			Keokuk YMCA	1S, 1D
West Suburban YMCA	1S*		**Marshalltown**	
Lake Forest			Marshalltown YMCA	2D
Onwentsia Club	1S, 1D		**Mount Vernon**	
Mount Vernon			Cornell College	1S, 1D
Mt. Vernon YMCA	1S*		**Ottumwa**	
Naperville			YMCA	2D
Naperville YMCA	1S*			
Niles			**KANSAS**	
†Leaning Tower YMCA	1S		Fort Leavenworth	3S, 3D
Northbrook			Fort Riley	4S
†North Suburban YMCA	1S		MacDonnell A.F.B.	2S, 2D
Peoria			**Wichita**	
Peoria YMCA	1S, 1D		†Shillelagh Inn	1S
Rockford				
Rockford YMCA	1S*		**KENTUCKY**	
Rolling Meadows			**Berea**	
Gould Sports Complex— Meadow Club	2S, 1D		Berea College	1S
			Lexington	
			†High Street Branch YMCA	2S*
			W. T. Storage Co.	1S
			Louisville	
INDIANA			Louisville Jewish Community Center	4S*
Culver			†Pendennis Club	3S
Culver Military Academy	4S, 2S*		Suburban Doctors Club	1S
Elkhart			**Owensboro**	
Elkhart YMCA	1S*		Family Y of Owensboro	2S, 2S*
Fort Wayne				
Fort Wayne Central YMCA	1S*		**LOUISIANA**	
Hammond			*Barksdale AFB*	1S
Hammond Area YMCA	1S*		**Baton Rouge**	
Indianapolis			Louisiana State University	1S
Indianapolis Athletic Club	4S, 2D		*Fort Polk*	2S
Jordan Branch of Greater Indianapolis	1S		**Lake Charles**	
University Club	2S		†Lake Charles YMCA	2S*

New Orleans
Naval Air Station   1S*

MAINE
Augusta
Kennebec Valley YMCA   2S*
Bangor
Bangor YMCA   2S*
Brunswick
Bowdoin College   10S, 1D
Castine
Maine Maritime Academy   1S, 1D
Limestone
Loring AFB   2S
Orono
University of Maine   1D
Portland
†Portland YMCA   2S
University of Maine   1S
Presque Isle
USAF Missile Base   1S
Waterville
†Colby College   8S, 1D

MARYLAND
Aberdeen Proving Ground   2S
Annapolis
St. John's College   2S*
U.S. Naval Academy   27S
Baltimore
Baltimore Country Club   2S, 1D
Jewish Community Center   3S*
Johns Hopkins University   5S
Maryland Club   4S, 1D
The Racquet Club   2S, 1D
Roland Park Gymnasium   2S
Terra Management Co.   2S, 1D
Bel Air
†Deitz Squash Club   1S
private court   1S
Bethesda
Potomac Squash Club   2S, 1D
College Park
University of Maryland   2S
Columbia
†Columbia Athletic Club   2S, 1D
Fort George Meade   3S
Lutherville
Green Spring Racquet Club   2S
Potomac
Seven Locks Athletic Club   2S, 1D
Rockville
Jewish Community Center of
    Greater Washington   1S
Towson
Towson State University   4S, 2D

Towson YMCA   2S
MASSACHUSETTS
Amherst
Amherst College   8S, 2D
University of Mass.   5S
Andover
Phillips Academy   8S
Attleboro
YMCA   2S
Babson Park
Babson Institute   2S
Belmont
Belmont Hill School   2S
Beverly
Beverly YMCA   1S, 1S*
Boston
Boston Army Base   2S
Boston State College   3S
†Boston YMCA   4S
Downtown Athletic Club   2S
Harvard Club   11S, 1D
Northeastern University   4S*
†Tennis & Racquet Club   7S
Union Boat Club   7S
University Club of Boston   9S
University of Mass.—Boston   2S
Brockton
Men's Division—Old Colony
    YMCA   2S*
Brookline
Brookline School   1S
Cambridge
Cambridge YMCA   2S
Harvard University   8S, 37S*
Harvard Medical School   5S
Massachusetts Institute of
    Technology   16S
Cape Anne
YMCA   1S
Chestnut Hill
Boston College   3S
Sidney Hill Country Club   1S
private court   1S*
Cohasset
Cohasset Tennis & Squash   1S
Concord
Concord-Acton Squash Club   4S
Middlesex School   4S
private court   1S
Deerfield
Deerfield Academy   5S
Dover
private court   1S
Easthampton
Williston-Northampton School   3S

Fall River		Springfield College	4S*
†Greater Fall River YMCA	2S	Springfield J.C.C.	1S
Falmouth		**Swampscott**	
†Falmouth Sports Center	1S	YMCA	1S
Groton		**Waltham**	
Groton School	4S	†Brandeis University	2S
Lawrence Academy	2S*	Waltham Racquet Club	1S
Haverhill		**Wayland**	
Haverhill YMCA	2S*	private court	1S
Holyoke		**Wellesley**	
Holyoke YMCA	1S	Maugus Club	2S
Hopedale		Wellesley College	2S
private court	1S	**Westfield**	
Littleton		Westfield YMCA	1S
private court	1S	**Weston**	
Lowell		Weston Golf Club	2S
Lowell Tech. Institute	3S	Wightman Tennis Center	2S
Marblehead		**Williamstown**	
Marblehead YMCA	1S	Williams College	14S, 1D
Marion		**Worcester**	
Tabor Academy	4S	Clark University	1S*
Medford		†Worcester Central YMCA	2S
Tufts University	6S	Worcester Jewish Community	
Milton		Center	1S
Milton Academy	3S		
Milton Hoosic Club	2S	**MICHIGAN**	
Needham		**Ann Arbor**	
Needham YMCA	1S	Ann Arbor Squash Club (Univ.	
Newton		of Mich.)	18S
Newton Squash-Tennis Club	2S	**Bay City**	
Newton YMCA	2S	Bay City YMCA	1S*
North Adams		**Birmingham**	
State College	1S	Birmingham Athletic Club	5S, 1D
Northampton		Birmingham Branch YMCA	1S*
Smith College	6S	private court	1S
North Andover		**Bloomfield**	
Brooks School	5S	Indian Mound	1S
Merrimack College	2S	**Detroit**	
private court	1S	Detroit Athletic Club	5S
Northfield		Detroit Racquet Club	3S
Otis AFB	1S	Detroit Tennis Club	2S
Pittsfield		†Eastside Branch YMCA	2S
†Pittsfield Jewish Community		Hannan Branch YMCA	2S*
Center	1S	Henry Ford Hospital	2S*
Pittsfield YMCA	1S*	private court	1S
Salem		Sidney-Hill Downtown Club	3S
North Shore Tennis & Squash Club	1S	Strathcona Club	1S
Salem State College	4S*	University Club of Detroit	4S, 1D
Sheffield		Uptown Athletic Club	6S
Berkshire School	2S	Wayne State University	6S
Southborough		Western YMCA	2S
Fay School	1S	†YMCA of Metropolitan Detroit	4S*
St. Mark's School	2S	**East Lansing**	
Springfield		Michigan State University	
Springfield Central YMCA	2S	Squash Club	4S
		Farmington	
		Detroit Tennis & Squash Club	2S

Flint
†Flint YMCA   1S
Grand Rapids
†Central Branch Grand Rapids
  YMCA   1S*
private court   1S
Grosse Pointe Shores
private court   1S
private court   1S*
Kalamazoo
†Kalamazoo YMCA   1S
Lansing
Lansing YMCA   2S*
Michigan State University   6S
Midland
Midland Community Center   2S
Mt. Clemens
Macomb YMCA   2S*
Muskegon
Family Christian Association   1S
Rochester
Oakland University   1S
Royal Oak
Red Run Country Club   1S
South Oakland Branch (YMCA)   1S*
Saginaw
private court   1S
Sawyer AFB   1S
Southfield
†Southfield Athletic Club   6S, 2D
West Bloomfield
Jewish Community Center of
  Metro. Detroit   4S, 1D
Wurthsmith AFB   1S, 1D

MINNESOTA
Bloomington
Decathlon A.C.   2S
Duluth
Dep't. of the Air Force (Duluth
  Int. Airport)   1S
Duluth YMCA   1S*
Gitche-gumee Club   2S*
Mankato
Mankato State   2S
Minneapolis
Calhoun Beach Club   2S
J.C.C.   1S
Minneapolis Athletic Club   2S
Minneapolis Club   2S, 1D
University of Minnesota   8S
Northfield
Carleton College   5S*
St. Paul
Arden Hill Club   1S

College of St. Thomas   2S
†Commodore Squash Racquet
  Club   2S, 1D
St. Paul Athletic Club   2S
University Club   2S
Winona
St. Mary's College   4S*
Winona YMCA   4S*

MISSISSIPPI
Biloxi
Keesler Air Force Base   1S
Columbus AFB   1S
Hattiesburg
Hattiesburg YMCA   1S
Meridian
†Naval Air Station   1S

MISSOURI
Columbia
University of Missouri—Columbia   2S*
Kansas City
Downtown YMCA   1S
Kansas City Athletic Club   1S
Pembroke C. D. School   4S
University Club   3S
University of Missouri (K.C.)   3S, 2S*
Maryville
Northwest Missouri State   2S
Richmond Height
†The University Club of
  St. Louis   2S, 1D
St. Joseph
St. Joeseph YMCA   2S*
St. Louis
Downtown YMCA Health Center   1S*
Jewish Community Centers
  Association   4S
Media Club   2S
Missouri Athletic Club   2S, 1D
Northside Branch YMCA   2S
Racquet Club of St. Louis   2S, 2D
Thomas Jefferson School   1S
Town & Country
Town & Country Tennis Club   1S
MONTANA
Butte
Butte YMCA   1S*
Great Falls
Great Falls Family YMCA   2S*
Libby
Libby Racquet Club   1S*
Malmstrom AFB   1S*

NEBRASKA
Grand Island
†Grand Island YMCA   1S*

Lincoln
Lincoln Central YMCA	1S*
†Lincoln University Club	2S*
University of Nebraska	9S*
Offutt Air Force Base	3S

Omaha
Central YMCA	1S
Omaha Club	2S
West Roads	1S

York
†Community Center	1S

NEVADA
Nellis AFB	1S, 2S*

Reno
YMCA of Reno	2S

NEW HAMPSHIRE

Concord
Bow Brook	2S
Concord YMCA	1S
St. Paul's School	8S

Dublin
Dublin School	2S

Exeter
†Phillips Exeter Academy	12S

Franconia
†White Mountain School	2S

Hanover
Dartmouth College	10S, 1D

Keene
Amalgamated Squash, Chowder & Devel. Corp.	1S*
Keene YMCA	2S*

Manchester
†The Manchester Court Club	2S

Milford
†Hampshire Hills Racquet & Health Club	2S

Nashua
†YMCA	1S

NEW JERSEY

Atlantic City
Haddon Hall Racquet Club	2S

Bergenfield
Bergenfield-Dumont J.C.C.	1S, 1D

Bogota
Bogota Racquet Club	2S

Camden
Central YMCA	1S

Chatham
Chatham Squash Club	6S

Elizabeth
Elizabeth Town & Country Club	1S

Englewood
Englewood Field Club	2S

Fort Lee
†Fort Lee Racquet Club	2S

Franklin Lakes
Franklin Lake Indian Trail Club	1S

Hoboken
Stevens Institute of Technology	4S

Madison
Drew University	2S

Mahwah
†The Tennis Barn	3S
McGuire AFB	2S

Montclair
Montclair Racquets Club	1S
†Montclair YMCA	2S

Newark
Essex Club	2S
Newark YM-YWCA	1S*

New Brunswick
Rutgers University	4S

Orange
Orange Central YMCA	2S*

Paterson
Paterson Branch YMCA	1S
Paterson YM-YWHA	1S

Plainfield
Plainfield Area YMCA	2S
Plainfield Country Club	2S

Princeton
Pretty Brook Tennis Club	2S
Princeton University	30S, 2D
Princeton YMCA	2S*

Ridgewood
private court	1S

Seabright
Seabright B & S Club	1S, 1D

Short Hills
Racquets Club	2S
Short Hills Club	2S

Somerville
Raritan Valley Country Club	2S

South Orange
Seton Hall University	2S

Summit
Summit Area YMCA	1S*

Teaneck
Teaneck Tennis & Squash Club	3S

Trenton
†The Trenton Club	2S
YMCA Trenton	2S

Wayne
J.C.C.	2S*
YM-YWHA of North Jersey	2S

NEW MEXICO

Albuquerque
Sandia Base	1S
Tennis Club of Albuquerque	2S, 2S*
University of New Mexico	4S*

Kirtland AFB | 2S

Los Alamos
†Los Alamos Family YMCA	2S

Roswell
Roswell Family YMCA	2S*

Sante Fe
The Kiva Club	2S, 1D

NEW YORK

Albany
Albany YMCA	2S*

Alfred
Alfred University	4S

Annandale-on-Hudson
Bard College	1S

Ardsley-on-Hudson
Ardsley Country Club	2S

Auburn
Auburn YMCA	2S

Batavia
Batavia YMCA	3S, 1S*

Bayside
North Shore Tennis & Racquets Club	2S

Binghamton
Binghamton YMCA	1S

Bridgehampton
private court	1S

Bronxville
Bronxville Field Club	2S
Concordia College	2S

Brookville
Long Island University	1S
Post (C. W.) College	1S

Buffalo
†Buffalo Athletic Club	2S, 1S*
The Buffalo Club	3S
Buffalo Tennis & Squash Club	5S, 2D
Canisius College	2S, 2S*
Downtown Branch YMCA	1S
Montefiore Club	2S, 1D
Nichols School	2S
†Saturn Club	3S
University of Buffalo	2S
University Club	4S

Canton
St. Lawrence University	8S

Cedarhurst
The Rockaway Hunt Club	4S, 1D

Clinton
Hamilton College	4S

Cooperstown
†Alfred Corning Clark Gymnasium	2S*

Corning
Corning Country Club	1S

Cortland
Cortland State University	8S

Elmira
Elmira College	6S

Flushing
†Flushing YMCA	1S, 1D

Garden City
Adelphi College	2S

Garrison
The Malcolm Gordon School	1S

Geneva
Hobart College	3S

Glen Cove
Nassau Country Club	2S, 1D

Hamilton
Colgate University	1S*

Ithaca
Cornell University	13S

Jamestown
YMCA	1S*

Kingston
†YMCA	4S*

Lake Placid
Lake Placid Club	2S

Locust Valley
Piping Rock Club	1S, 1D

Macedon
private court	1S

Mamaroneck
†Squash/1	5S

Manhasset
Shelter Rock Tennis Club	2S

Mount Kisco
†Saw Mill River Courts	1S

Newburgh
†Newburgh YMCA	2S*

New Rochelle
Huguenot YMCA	2S*

New York City

Bronx
Bronx Union YMCA	1S*
Century Towers	2S
Fordham University	5S
Riverdale Yacht Club	2S

Brooklyn
Brooklyn College	2S, 6S*
Brooklyn Crescent Club	3S
Brooklyn Naval Station	2S
Flatbush Jewish Center	2S
Heights Casino	2S, 1D

Poly Prep. School 4S
SUNY–Downstate Medical Center 2S
Union Temple 2S
Manhattan
†Broad Street Squash Club 8S, 1E
City Athletic Club 4S*, 1D
Columbia Presby. Med. Ctr. 4S
Columbia University 17S
Downtown Athletic Club 9S
Fifth Ave. Racquet Club 7S
Harmonie Club 3S
Harvard Club 6S, 2S*
Lone Star Boat Club 2S
†Manhattan Squash Club 10S, 2S*, 1D
New York Athletic Club 5S, 1S*
New York Health Club 2S
New York University 3S
†Park Avenue Squash and
  Racquet Club 10S
†Park Place Squash Club 4S, 1E
Princeton Club 3S
Racquet and Tennis Club 5S, 1D
River Club 1S
St. Bartholomew's Church 1S
Seventh Regiment Squash Club 2S*
†Turtle Bay Racquet Club 4S
Union Club 3S, 1D
Union League Club 3S
U.S. Naval Communications
  Station 1S*
University Club 7S, 1D
†Uptown Racquet Club 12S, 2E
Yale Club 5S
†West Side YMCA 2S
YMCA (840 8th Avenue) 2S, 1S*
Private Court 1S
Norwich
Norwich YMCA 1S
Oceanside
†Point-Set Indoor Racquet Club 1S
Olean
St. Bonaventure University 1S
Oneonta
Oneonta State College 4S
Oswego
Oswego College 4S
Pawling
Trinity-Pawling School 4S
Port Chester
Port Chester YMCA 2S*
Poughkeepsie
†Poughkeepsie Squash Club 1S
Vassar College 4S
Rochester
Genesee Valley Club 4S, 1D
Kodak Park 2S
Midtown Tennis Club 2S

†Midtown YMCA 3S
University Club 2S*
University of Rochester 5S
University of Rochester–
  Medical Center 4S
Rye
Apawamis Club 2S, 1D
Rye Squash Barn 1S
Westchester Country Club 1S
Saratoga Springs
†Saratoga County Y 2S
Scarborough-on-Hudson
Sleepy Hollow C. C. 2S, 1D
Scarsdale
Mid-Westchester YMHA 2S
Schenectady
†Schenectady County YMCA 2S*
Southampton
Meadow Club 1S
Spring Glen
Homowack Lodge 1D
Staten Island
Wagner College 2S
Stony Brook
State University of New York 4S
Syracuse
Syracuse Jewish Community
  Center 1S
Syracuse YMCA 2S
University Club 1S*
Troy
Rensselaer Polytechnic Institute 5S*
Utica
Utica YMCA 1S
West Amherst
†Jewish Center of Greater Buffalo 1S
West Point
†United States Military Academy 21S
White Plains
White Plains YMCA 1S*
Yonkers
Yonkers YMCA 1S

NORTH CAROLINA
†*Camp Lejeune* 1S, 1S*
Charlotte
†Charlotte Country Club 2S
Durham
Duke University 2S*
Fort Bragg 2S
Greensboro
†Greensboro Central YMCA 1S*
High Point
High Point YMCA 2S*

Raleigh
North Carolina State — 6S
St. Augustine's College — 2S
Statesville
†YMCA of Iredell-Statesville — 2S*
Wilmington
Wilmington YMCA — 1S*
Winston Salem
Wake Forest College — 10S
†Winston Salem Central YMCA — 3S

NORTH DAKOTA
Fargo
Fargo-Moorhead YMCA — 2S*
Grand Forks
Dept. of the Air Force — 2S
University of North Dakota — 2S, 1S*

OHIO
Ada
Ohio Northern University — 2S*
Akron
†Akron Central YMCA — 1D
Bowling Green
Bowling Green State University — 4S, 2S*
Bucyrus
Bucyrus YMCA — 2S*
Canton
Malone College Athletics — 1S
private court — 1S
Cincinnati
Central Parkway YMCA — 2S*
†Cincinnati Country Club — 2S, 1D
†Cincinnati Racquet Club — 2S
Glendale Lyceum — 1S
University of Cincinnati — 2S*
University Club — 2S
Cleveland
Case Western Reserve University — 2S
Cleveland Athletic Club — 2S, 2S*
Cleveland Central YMCA — 3S*
Cleveland State University — 2S
Oakwood Country Club — 2S
Tavern Club — 3S
University Circle YMCA — 1S*
University Club of Cleveland — 4S
Cleveland Heights
Jewish Community Center — 1S
Columbus
Athletic Club of Columbus — 2S
Columbus Central YMCA — 1S*
Ohio State University — 6S*
University Club — 1D
Dayton
†Central YMCA — 2S
Dayton Racquet Club — 2S
Wright-Patterson AFB — 2S

Wright State University — 4S
Delaware
Ohio Wesleyan University — 1S
Findlay
Findlay YMCA — 1S*
Fostoria
†YMCA — 1S*
Hamilton
Hamilton YMCA — 1S*
Hiram
Hiram College — 1S, 2D
Hudson
Western Reserve Academy — 2S*
Lima
Lima YMCA — 1S*
Mansfield
Mansfield YMCA — 1S
Massillon
Masillon YMCA — 2S*
Mayfield Village
Mayfield Village Racquet Club — 2S
Middletown
Middletown YMCA — 3S*
Mount Vernon
†Mount Vernon YMCA — 2S*
Oberlin
Oberlin College — 6S, 1D
Painesville
Lake County YMCA — 3S
Pepper Pike
†Cleveland Racquet Club — 3S*, 1D
Piqua
Piqua YMCA — 2S*
Springfield
Springfield YMCA — 1S
Toledo
Shadow Valley — 4S, 1D
Toledo Club — 5S
Toledo YMCA — 3S*
Warren
Warren YMCA — 1S
Wilmington
Wilmington College — 2S
Youngstown
Jewish Community Center — 1S*
†YMCA — 3S
Youngstown State University — 2S
Zanesville
Zanesville YMCA — 1S*

OKLAHOMA
Oklahoma City
†YMCA of Oklahoma City — 1S
Tulsa
Tulsa Club — 1S

Tulsa YMCA   1S*

OREGON

Corvallis
Oregon State University   2S

Eugene
†Central Lane County YMCA   1S
University of Oregon   8S*

Forest Grove
Pacific University   1S

Lake Oswego
Mountain Park Racquet Club   1S

Monmouth
Oregon College of Education   2S*

Portland
Air Guard Base   1S*
Lewis & Clark College   2S, 1D
Multnomah Athletic Club   9S, 1D
Portland State University   2D
Portland YMCA   2S
Racquet Club of Portland   2S*
Reed College   3S, 1D
University of Oregon
    Medical School   1S
private court   1S

PENNSYLVANIA

Bala-Cynwyd
Cynwyd Club   2S, 2S*, 1D

Berwyn
†Berwyn Squash Racquets
    Club   5S, 1D
Upper Mainline YMCA   2S

Bethlehem
Saucon Valley Country Club   2S, 1D

Bradford
Bradford YMCA   2S*

Butler
Butler YMCA   1S, 1D

Carlisle
Carlisle Barracks   2S*
†Carlisle YMCA   1S
Dickinson College   2S

Chambersburg
†Chambersburg YMCA   2S

Chester Springs
Ship Valley Squash Racquets
    Ass'n.   1D

Coatesville
Coatesville YMCA   2S

Collegeville
Ursinus College   2S*

East Stroudsburg
East Stroudsburg State College   1S, 2S*

Erie
†Erie YMCA   2S*

Fairless Hills
†Lower Bucks County YMCA   2S*

Gladwyne
Philadelphia Country Club   2S, 1D

Greensburg
Greensburg YMCA   1S*
private court   1S

Grove City
Grove City College   2S*

Harrisburg
Central YMCA   2S

Haverford
Haverford School   4S
Merion Cricket Club   5S, 2S*, 2D

Hazleton
Hazleton YMCA   1S*

Huntingdon Valley
Huntingdon Valley Country Club   2S

King of Prussia
†Sheraton-Valley Forge   1S

Lancaster
Franklin & Marshall College   4S
Hamilton Club   2S
†Lancaster YMCA   2S

Latrobe
Latrobe Borough   1S*

Lewisburg
Bucknell University   4S

Meadville
Allegheny College   5S, 1D

Mercersburg
Mercersburg Academy   8S

Merion
Episcopal Academy   4S

Monroeville
†The Racquet Club   4S

New Castle
New Castle YMCA   2S*

North Wales
Gwynedd Racquet Club   2S, 1D
private court   1S

Philadelphia
Central Branch YMCA   1S
Chestnut Hill Academy   3S
Drexel Institute of Technology   5S
Germantown Cricket Club   2S, 3S*, 1D
Germantown YMCA   1S*
Navy Aviation Supply Office   1S
Northeast Racquet Club   2S
Philadelphia Cricket Club   2S, 2D
Princeton Club   2S
Racquet Club   2S, 1D
†Schuylkill Courts   7S
University of Penn.   23S, 1D
†Washington Square Courts   5S
West Village Squash Club   2S, 1D

Wm. Penn Charter School	3S, 1D

Phoenixville
†Phoenixville Area YMCA — 1S

Pittsburgh
Carnegie Inst. of Tech. — 2S*
Golden Triangle YMCA — 1S, 2S*
†J.C.C. — 4S
Pittsburgh Athletic Association — 3S, 1D
Pittsburgh Golf Club — 2S, 1D
Shady Side Academy — 4S, 1D
†University Club of Pittsburgh — 2S
University of Pittsburgh — 8S

Pottstown
The Hill School — 4S
Pottstown YMCA — 1S

Reading
Reading Co. YMCA
 (R. R. YMCA) — 1S*
Reading YMCA — 1S

Scranton
J.C.C. — 2S*
Scranton — 1S*

Sewickley
Edgeworth Club — 2S
Sewickley YMCA — 2S*

Shippensburg
Shippensburg State — 4S

Slippery Rock
Slippery Rock State College — 1S*

Springfield
Victoria Tennis Club — 2S

Swarthmore
Swarthmore College — 5S, 1D

University Park
The Pennsylvania State University — 16S

Warren
†Warren YMCA — 1S*

West Chester
West Chester YMCA — 1S*

Westtown
South Penn Wood Squash
 Racquets Ass'n. — 1D

Wilkes-Barre
Wilkes-Barre YMCA — 1S, 1S*
Wyoming Valley Squash
 Racquets Club — 2S

Williamsport
Williamsport YMCA — 1S, 1S*

Youngwood
Dickerson Enterprises — 1S

York
York YMCA — 2S

RHODE ISLAND

Barrington
Rhode Island Country Club — 2S

Cranston
Cranston YMCA — 1S

Kingston
University of Rhode Island — 2S*

Newport
Naval Education and Training
 Center — 2S
†Newport Squash Racquets — 3S
Newport YMCA — 1S

Pawtucket
†Pawtucket YMCA — 2S, 1S*

Portsmouth
Portsmouth Priory School — 2S

Providence
Agawam Hunt Club — 2S
Brown University — 4S
Hope Club — 1S
†Providence Central YMCA — 2S
Providence College — 3S
Rhode Island Country Club — 4S
†Rhode Island Hospital — 1S
The University Club — 2S

Warwick
Kent County YMCA — 2S*

SOUTH CAROLINA

Aiken
Aiken Prep. School — 2S

Charleston
private court — 1S

Columbia
Columbia YMCA — 3S

Greenville
†Washington Park Squash Club — 2S
YMCA of Greater Greenville — 1S
Shaw Air Force Base — 1D

Spartanburg
†The Racquet Club — 1S
Spartanburg Squash Club — 2S*
Spartanburg YMCA — 2S*

SOUTH DAKOTA

Ellsworth Air Force Base — 2S

Sioux Falls
Sioux Falls YMCA — 1S*

TENNESSEE

Chattanooga
†Chattanooga YMCA — 1S

Knoxville
†Central Branch YMCA — 1S*

Memphis
J.C.C. — 1S*

Manufacturers Country Club	1S
Memphis Country Club	1S, 1S*
Naval Air Station	2S
University Club	2S
Oak Ridge	
Golf & Country Club	1S

TEXAS
Abilene
Dyess AFB	1S

Amarillo
YMCA	1D

Austin
St. Edward's University	3S
†University of Texas at Austin	14S, 7S*
Chase Field NAS	1S, 1D
†Bergstrom AFB	1S
Brooks AFB	1D
Carswell AFB	1S

Corsicana
Corsicana YMCA	1S*

Dallas
Dallas Athletic Club	2S*
Downtown YMCA	1S
†Inwood Racquet Club	2S
Fort Hood	3S, 1D

Houston
†Downtown Y	2S*
Metropolitan Racquet Club	2S
Rice University	2S*
University Club of Houston	2S

Midland
Midland YMCA	2S*
W. R. Appleby Inc.	1S
private courts	3S
†Randolph Air Force Base	1S
Webb Air Force Base	1S

UTAH
Hill AFB	2S*

Logan
†Sherwood Hills	1S

Ogden
Deseret Gymnasium	1S*

Provo
Brigham Young University	2S

Salt Lake City
Chancellor Club	1S
Deseret Gymnasium	4S, 1D
Salt Lake Athletic Club	1S*
†YMCA	1S

VERMONT
Burlington
Burlington YMCA	1S

University of Vermont	2S, 1S*

Lyndon
Lyndon State College	1S

Middlebury
Middlebury College	6S, 1D

Quechee
Quechee Club	2S

Rutland
Rutland Indoor Tennis Club	1S

South Burlington
†The Court Club	2S

Stowe
Snowflake Motor Inn	1S

Waitsfield
The Bridges	2S

VIRGINIA
Alexandria
Episcopal High School	2S*

Arlington
†Arlington "Y" Tennis & Squash Club	2S

Blacksburg
Va. Polytech. Inst.	2S

Charlottesville
†Albemarle Racquet Club	2S
Boar's Head Sports	3S, 1D
University of Virginia	8S

Fairfax
†The Courts Royal	2S
Fort Belvoir	4S
†Fort Monroe—YMCA on Post	1S*

Harrisonburg
Madison College	3S*
†Langley AFB	2S

Lexington
Washington & Lee University	2S*

Lynchburg
Lynchburg Science Building	2S
Lynchburg Squash Club	2S

McLean
Regency Racquet Club	4S, 1S*

Norfolk
J.C.C.	1S*
Naval Amphibious Base	3S
Norfolk YMCA	1S*
Norfolk Yacht and Country Club	2S

Reston
Reston G & C C	2S*

Richmond
Bellwood Depot	1S
Central YMCA	1S*
Medical College of Virginia	2S
Univ. of Richmond	2S

Westwood Racquet Club	2S	**WEST VIRGINIA**	
Roanoke		**Bethany**	
private court	1S	Bethany College	1S
Virginia Beach		**Charleston**	
FCDSTC, Dam Neck	1S*	Edgewood Country Club	2S
Woodberry Forest		**Daniels**	
Woodberry Forest School	1S	Glade Springs	1S, 1D
		Huntington	
		Huntington YMCA	2S*
		Morgantown	
WASHINGTON		West Virginia University	2S
Bellevue		West Virginia University Coliseum	2S*
private court	1S	**Wheeling**	
Bellingham		†YMCA	1S*
Bellingham YMCA	1S		
Bremerton		**WISCONSIN**	
†Bremerton Armed Services YMCA	2S	**Appleton**	
Cheney		Appleton Family YMCA	2S*
Eastern Washington State College	1S*	**Beloit**	
Everett		Beloit YMCA	1D
B.P.O. Elks #479	1S	**Fond Du Lac**	
Fairchild AFB	1S	Fond Du Lac YMCA	2S*
Kirkland		**LaCrosse**	
Center Park Racquet Club	2S	Wisconsin State University	3S*
Mercer Island		**Madison**	
private court	1S	Central YMCA	1S, 1D
Oak Harbor		†University of Wisconsin	5S, 1D
NAS Whidbey Island	1S, 1D	**Milwaukee**	
Port Ludlow		Milwaukee Athletic Club	3S, 1D
Port Ludlow resort	1S	Milwaukee Central YMCA	1S
Seattle		†Milwaukee J.C.C.	1S
College Club	2S	University Club	2S
Gallery Court & Racquet Club	1S	University School	1S
Lakeside School	2S	**New Richmond**	
†Seattle Downtown YMCA	3S	private court	1S
Seattle Tennis Club	3S	**Oshkosh**	
Seattle University	2S	Oshkosh Community YMCA	1S*
†Special Services—NAVSTA	1S*	**Racine**	
Tennis World of Seattle 6S, 1E, 1D		Racine Squash Club	1S
University of Washington	8S	Racine YMCA	1S
Washington Athletic Club	4S	**River Falls**	
Spokane		Wisconsin State	2S
†The Spokane Club	2S	**Wausau**	
Spokane YMCA	1S	Woodson YMCA	2S*
private court	1S	**Whitefish Bay**	
Tacoma		University School of Milwaukee	1S
Lakewood Racquet Club	1S		
McChord AFB	1S	**WYOMING**	
Pacific Lutheran University	1S	**Casper**	
Tacoma Lawn Tennis Club	2S	YMCA	1S*
Walla Walla		**Cheyenne**	
Walla Walla YMCA	1S*	†Cheyenne Family YMCA	1S
Whitman College	1S	F. E. Warren AFB	1S*
Wenatchee		**Laramie**	
Wenatchee YMCA	1S*	University of Wyoming	2S*